CAMPAIGN SERIES　35

PLASSEY 1757

GENERAL EDITOR DAVID G. CHANDLER

OSPREY MILITARY

CAMPAIGN SERIES 35

PLASSEY 1757

CLIVE OF INDIA'S FINEST HOUR

PETER HARRINGTON

Robert, first Baron Clive of Plassey, 1725–1774, one of the great heroes of the British Empire. His victory at Plassey, won against enormous odds, secured Bengal and set the British on the road to the conquest of India. This statue, standing at the eastern end of King Charles Street in the heart of Westminster, looks out across the lake, trees and greenery of St. James's Park. (DAG)

First published in Great Britain in 1994 by OSPREY, an imprint of Reed Consumer Books Limited, Michelin House, 81 Fulham Road, London SW3 6RB and Auckland, Melbourne Singapore and Toronto.

ISBN 1-85532-352-4

Produced by DAG Publications Ltd for Osprey Publishing Ltd. Colour bird's eye view illustrations by Peter Harper. Cartography by Micromap. *Wargaming Plassey* by Ian Drury. Printed and bound in Hong Kong.

▲ *A Victorian representation of the meeting of Mir Jafar and Robert Clive after the battle of Plassey. As with other nineteenth century depictions of the events, this scene is more imaginary than fact. The Victorians had a fascination with the exotic Orient and the artist has clearly emphasised the costume and panoply of Mir Jafar and his entourage. (Anne S. K. Brown Military Collection, Brown University Library)*

CONTENTS

India During the Seven Years War

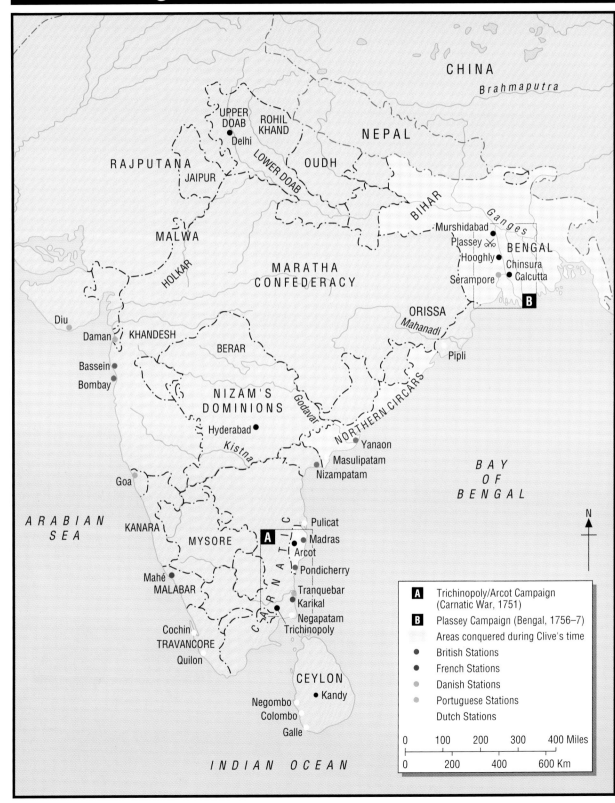

BACKGROUND TO PLASSEY

The road to Plassey can be traced back as far as the arrival of merchants from the East India Company in the 16th century. The Company had been founded in September 1599 at a meeting of the Lord Mayor of London and various aldermen and merchants who desired to have a piece of the lucrative trade the Dutch were enjoying in India. On 13 February 1601, five English ships under Captain James Lancaster set sail from Woolwich proclaiming the first trading venture with the sub-continent. The first port or factory was established at Surat by William Hawkins in 1612.

India at this time was ruled by the Great Moghul, and Sir Thomas Roe was made ambassador to the Moghul"s court. No treaty was signed, but by the time Roe left India three years later the English

▶ *The founding of Fort St. George in Madras by Francis Day, an officer of the East India Company in March 1639, from an illustration by Richard Caton Woodville, 1902 (Anne S. K. Brown Military Collection, Brown University Library).*

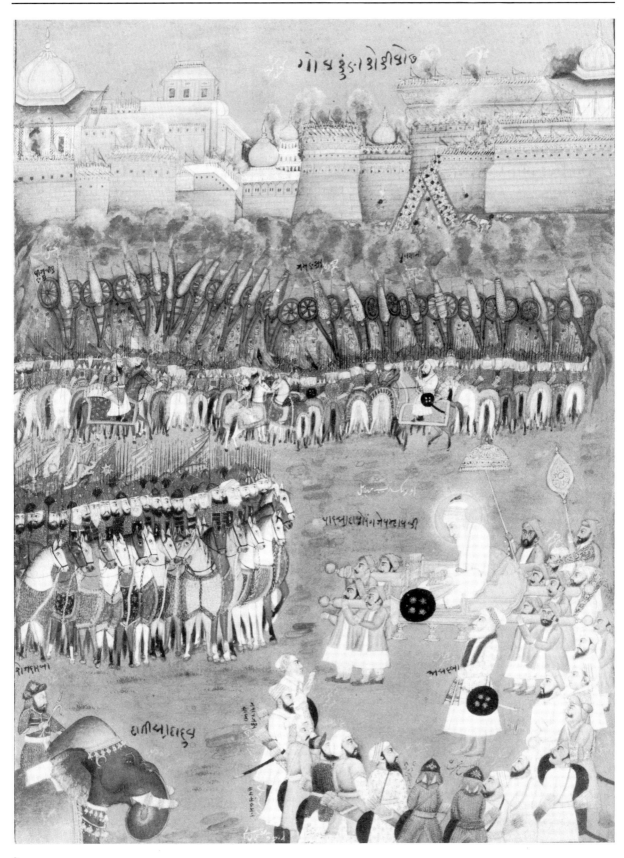

◀ *The Emperor Aurangzeb at the siege of Golconda in 1687. Gouache by a native artist. The Moghul Empire at the time consisted on 21 separate provinces of which fourteen were in Hindustan and six in the Deccan. Following the death of the Emperor in 1707, there was a period of intense internecine feuding over the succession which* *ended at the battle of Jajou near Agra in June 1707. Between 1707 and 1720, eight emperors were to reign briefly all but one of whom was to know a natural death. All this weakened the throne in the process, allowing foreign adventurers to move in. (Anne S. K. Brown Military Collection, Brown University Library)*

position in India was much better than it had been previously. This was at the expense of the Dutch, who resented their power being usurped. Throughout the 17th century, there were several brief clashes between the Dutch and the English, who had now established a major port at Fort St. George, the future Madras, in 1639. Upon the marriage of Charles II to Princess Catherine of Portugal in 1665, the island of Bombay was ceded to England. Later, Fort William on the Hooghly river was built.

By the early 18th century, Britain had a firm footing in India with Fort St. George at Madras on the south-east coast, Fort William at Calcutta in the east, and Bombay castle to the west. Each was a presidency independent of the others and controlled by a council of ten merchants and a president. In order to pursue a mercantile industry with the sub-continent, however, it was important to secure allies among the various princes, and consequently each presidency worked with the local native governors, or Nawabs, to gain concessions. The Nawabs often gave the British what they wanted in return for guarantees of security against any likely usurpers.

The Company had little interest in war, as the Directors pronounced in 1681: 'All war is so contrary to our interest that we cannot too often inculcate to you our aversion thereunto.' However, the employment of force was sometimes unavoidable as Company officials repeatedly created situations requiring soldiers and money from Britain. The great distance and the poor communications (sometimes up to a year before information was received) meant that local situations often got out of hand before the government in London could react. As a

consequence, the men on the spot wielded enormous power over the sensitive chain-drive of Indian politics. Added to this was the French involvement in the sub-continent. While France was a late-comer in the India trade, she was quickly gaining ground and could possible overtake Britain for control. While friction between the two was highly likely, it was their conflicts in Europe that spilled-over into India. In both the War of the Austrian Succession in the 1740s and the Seven Years War of the 1750s and 1760s, Britain and France opposed each other on the battlefield.

Anglo-French Hostilities

The first hostilities between the two European nations in India came in 1746, when a French fleet attacked and took Madras. To counter this, the British laid siege to the French trading port of Pondicherry. The upshot of these events was the restoration of Madras to Britain following the peace of 1748 in exchange for Louisbourg and Cape Breton Island in North America. The local French Governor, Dupleix, being the man on the spot and thousands of miles from Paris, took matters into his own hands. However, he chose to use a *local* power struggle to extend his influence. The feud was for the succession to two important positions – that of the Nizam of the Deccan, controlling on behalf of the Emperor a massive area lying between the south-west and south-east coasts; and the position of Nawab of the Carnatic, controlling the province of south-west India including the major European settlements of Madras and Pondicherry along the Coromandel coast and Trichinopoly. The French and British took opposing sides for the succession, nominating their own Indian candidates. With some manipulation and two assassinations, Dupleix's candidates were appointed to both thrones.

In mid-1751, a French force of 1,800 men under Charles, Marquis de Bussy, marched upon Trichinopoly to assist their confederate and claimant to the position of Nawab, Chanda Sahib, in besieging the British candidate for the Nawab's position, Mohammed Ali. In all, the Franco-Indian force numbered 8,000 men. The fall of Trichinopoly would spell the end of the East India Company's presence on the Coromandel Coast. A small group of council members had

The Carnatic Theatre of Operations, 1751

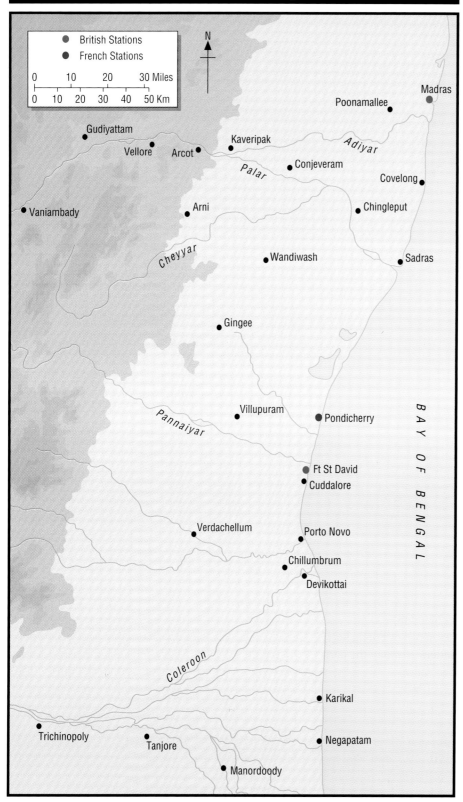

British Stations
French Stations

0   10   20   30 Miles
0 10 20 30 40 50 Km

N

Madras
Poonamallee
Gudiyattam
Kaveripak
Adiyar
Vellore   Arcot
Conjeveram
Palar
Covelong
Vaniambady
Arni
Chingleput
Cheyyar
Wandiwash
Sadras
Gingee
Villupuram
Pannaiyar
Pondicherry
Ft St David
Cuddalore
Verdachellum
Porto Novo
Chillumbrum
Devikottai
Coleroon
Karikal
Trichinopoly
Tanjore
Negapatam
Manordoody

BAY OF BENGAL

The Black Tow
entirely destroyed
Ditches filled by t
of M. Duplex

M

The Suburbs destr
by the French

▲ *A plan of Madras and the adjacent Fort St. George as it appeared in September 1746 when it was taken by the French under the Command of M. Mahe de la Bourdonnais. From an engraving by J. Cary published in 1781. (Anne S. K. Brown Military Collection, Brown University Library)*

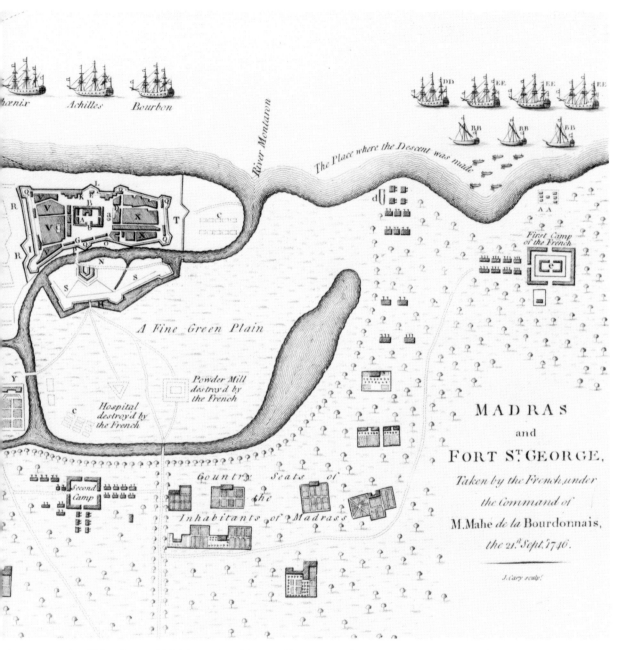

A Fine Green Plain

Powder Mill
destroy'd by
the French

Hospital
destroy'd by
the French

Country Seats of
the
Inhabitants of Madrass

First Camp
of the French

MADRAS
and
FORT St. GEORGE,
Taken by the French under
the Command of
M. Mahe de la Bourdonnais,
the 21.ᵈ Sept. 1746.

J. Cary sculp.ᵗ

Second
Camp

River Montauen

The Place where the Descent was made

been sent the 200 miles to Trichinopoly with supplies from Fort St. David, a few miles south of Pondicherry, by the Governor, Thomas Saunders . Among the party was a young officer named Robert Clive.

The small force managed to break through the French lines and reach the town. Clive, realising the predicament of the 1,600 strong garrison, returned to Fort St. David with twelve sepoys and another officer to inform the Governor of the situation and suggest a plan. While it might be impossible to relieve Trichinopoly, pressure could be taken off the town by

attacking an area owned by Chanda Sahib to force him to divert troops. In fact, while at Trichinopoly, Mohammed Ali had suggested such a place – Arcot, the capitol of the Carnatic, some 64 miles from Madras and home to Chanda Sahib's new palace.

Arcot

Arcot it was. The twenty-six year old Clive was to command a force of approximately 200 Europeans and 300 sepoys with three field pieces. On 22

◀ Portrait of Joseph-François, Marquis Dupleix, born in 1697, died in Paris in 1763. From a portrait by Ser- *gent engraved by Cernel in 1789. (Anne S. K. Brown Military Collection, Brown University Library)*

August 1751, the force sailed from Fort St. David to Madras, where it was joined by a further 80 European soldiers before commencing its march to Arcot. On 1 September, Arcot came into sight. Approaching the gate, they found to their astonishment that the garrison had fled the previous night – having heard of the dogged march lead by a fearless leader suggestive of some supernatural power. After hoisting Mohammed Ali's flag on the Nawab's palace in the name of the Moghul, Clive set about reinforcing the fort, in light of rumours of an impending attack from Chanda Sahib's son. He also led a successful attack upon the former garrison at midnight on the 14th. Two 18-pounders escorted by a few sepoys set out on the 16th for Arcot and, to

▶ *The Hon. Edward Boscawen, Admiral of the Blue Squadron of His Majesty's Fleet and one of the Lord's Commissioners of the Admiralty, 1758. Mezzotint. Shortly after the fall of Madras in 1746, the East India Company appealed to the government in London for help. It in turn dispatched Boscawen with a powerful squadron and over 2,000 troops. After arriving in August 1748, he set out with a combined force to besiege Pondicherry. Later in his career, he led the expedition to America in 1758 and was in command at the taking of Louisbourg. (Anne S. K. Brown Military Collection, Brown University Library)*

◀ *North west view of the King's Barracks and Parade, Fort-House and Church at Fort St. George, Madras, from an aquatint by J. Wells published in November 1788 from a drawing taken on the spot by Captain Trapaud. (Anne S. K. Brown Military Collection, Brown University Library)*

guarantee their safe arrival, Clive dispatched most of the garrison to escort them in. A strong enemy force in the vicinity of Conjeveram were aware of this and decided to attack Arcot while the garrison was weakened. Despite two concerted efforts, the Indian force was beaten off and the convoy arrived safely with the rest of the garrison.

In the meantime, Chanda Sahib took the bait and dispatched a force of 4,000 Indians under Raza Sahib and 150 Frenchmen under Du Saussay to Arcot. The garrison withdrew into the fort, allowing the enemy to enter the town on the night of 23 September. On the following day, Clive led a sortie and there was an artillery duel in the narrow streets in which most of the French gunners were killed. However, the Anglo-Indian troops were forced back into the fort, having lost fifteen Europeans and almost losing Clive in the process. With the arrival of additional troops, Raza Sahib besieged the fort. Raza had been reinforced by Mortazi Ali, who communicated to Clive that if the latter would come out and attack Raza, Mortazi would come over to his side. Clive mistrusted him and merely pretended to accept the offer, but Mortazi soon realised the trick.

On 24 October, French troops who had recently arrived from Pondicherry began to bombard the

▲ *Dupleix at the siege of Pondicherry in 1748 from an illustration by Couturier. The Frenchman managed to hold off a regular siege by Boscawen in command of a combined army-navy force when monsoon rains flooded the British trenches. The force retreated, leaving 1,000 men dead. Shortly after, the Treaty of Aix-la-Chapelle gave Madras back to Britain, but the feuding with France continued unabated. (Anne S. K. Brown Military Collection, Brown University Library)*

▶ *South-east view of the rock of Trichinopoly from a drawing by Edward Orme in 1804 viewed from the fort. The town was located on the south bank of the Cauvery. Another fortress surmounted the rock. The town was the scene of three battles between the French and the British with their Indian supporters, in June 1752, July 1753 and October 1753. (Anne S. K. Brown Military Collection, Brown University Library)*

fort. Clive responded by digging earthworks and mounting a huge gun on top of a mound, from which he proceeded to fire at Raza's palace. Six days later, Clive received a message asking him to surrender the fort. Clive refused in the anticipation that Morari Rao, a Mahratta chief somewhat loyal to the British cause with a force of 6,000, was about to arrive. Fearing this, Raza Sahib attempted one final assault on 24 November, but this failed when his

▶ *Portrait of the young Robert Clive. Engraving by A. Walker. There are no known portraits of Clive prior to his victory at Plassey, but this picture certainly predates Nathaniel Dance's more famous formal portrait painted in 1770 when the soldier had achieved his fame and fortune. (Anne. S. K. Brown Military Collection, Brown University Library)*

armoured elephants were stampeded by the noise of the musketry. When all else failed, the Indian leader decided to cut his losses and raise the siege after 50 days, abandoning guns, ammunition and stores. Clive had succeeded against all odds and was now viewed in the eyes of many as invincible.

Arcot was a turning-point for British fortunes in the subcontinent. It led to a period of intense rivalry between France and Britain under the guise of aiding various Indian princes against each other. With the success at Arcot and at a number of other battles including Clive's first victory at Arni on 3 December 1751 and Conjeveram twelve days later, Britain secured the Carnatic, and its surrogate, Mohammed Ali, succeeded to the Nawabship upon the death of Chanda Sahib.

▲ *Clive at Conjeveram, where a French garrison had established themselves to intercept movement between Madras and Arcot. His artillery bombardment was sufficient encouragement for the French to leave.*

▶ *Above right: Clive at the siege of Arcot. This is one of the bas relief panels on the base of his statue in Westminster.*

▶ *Below right: A depiction of Clive firing one of the guns himself at the siege of Arcot, drawn by J. A. Skelton in 1905. Following the bombardment of the fort by French troops who had come to the assistance of Raza Sahib, Clive mounted a large gun on top of a mound and commenced*

firing upon Raza's palace. The final assault on 24 November 1751 was driven back by Clive's force and the siege was lifted. (Anne S. K. Brown Military Collection, Brown University Library)

The Bengal Theatre of Operations, 1756–1757

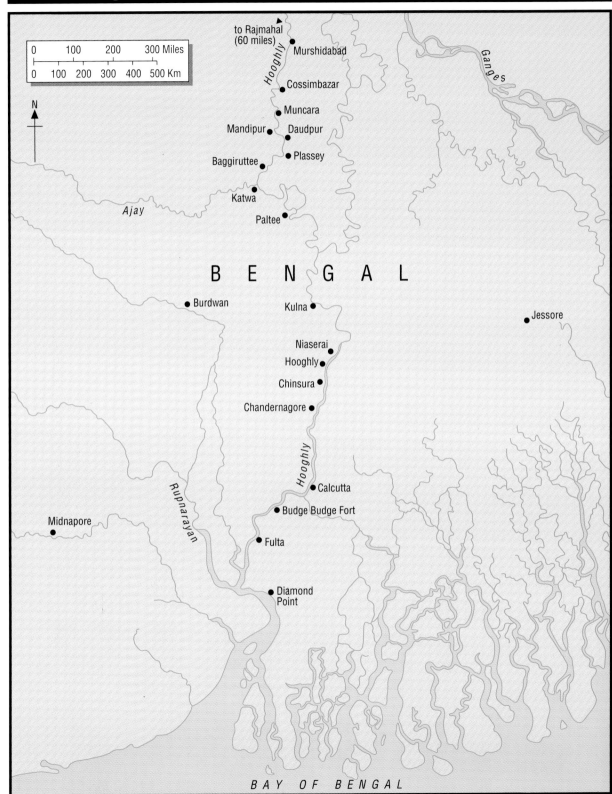

to Rajmahal
(60 miles)

Murshidabad

Cossimbazar

Muncara

Mandipur

Daudpur

Plassey

Baggiruttee

Katwa

Paltee

Ajay

B E N G A L

Burdwan

Kulna

Jessore

Niaserai

Hooghly

Chinsura

Chandernagore

Rupnarayan

Midnapore

Hooghly

Calcutta

Budge Budge Fort

Fulta

Diamond
Point

Hooghly

Ganges

N

0   100   200   300 Miles
0   100   200   300   400   500 Km

B A Y   O F   B E N G A L

CALCUTTA

Things were not going so well in Bengal. While trade had been progressing well throughout the 1750s, the death in 1756 of the Nawab, Aliverdi Khan, spelt trouble, for he was succeeded by his grandson Siraj-ud-daula, a hot-headed, greedy, arrogant man who was particularly suspicious of the Indian traders who ran Bengal. These were Mar-waris from Rajputana, and Siraj (rightly) suspected them of wanting to overthrow him. The young Nawab soon also became increasingly aware of the large profits the East India Company and other European companies were making and made plans to move against them. In anticipation of this, the French and British had started to strengthen their

▶ *Portrait of young Warren Hastings, engraved by T. Knight from a painting by Sir Joshua Reynolds. Hastings arrived in Bengal at the age of 17 in October 1750. After two years in Calcutta he was sent to Cossimbazar where he worked with native brokers. When it was seized by Siraj in 1756, he was arrested but was released shortly after. He joined Clive's expedition when it came up from Madras in December 1756 but realising the young man's diplomatic skills, Clive appointed him to be the resident agent at the court of the new Nawab, Mir Jafar, shortly after Plassey. In 1760 he joined the Council in Calcutta. He eventually became Governor-General of Bengal. (Anne S. K. Brown Military Collection, Brown University Library)*

▲ *Calcutta as it appeared in 1756. Engraving from Orme's* History. *The town suffered greatly throughout the 1740s and 1750s from fear of attack by various native chieftains. After*

Plassey, a period of peace descended upon the place which had now grown to a city with a population of more than 150,000 people. (Anne S. K. Brown Military Collection, Brown University Library)

▼ *Plan for the Intelligence of the Military Operations at Calcutta when attacked and taken by Siraj-ud-daula.' Engraving from Orme's* A History of the Military Transactions of the

British Nation *in Indostan published in 1778. (Anne S. K. Brown Military Collection, Brown University Library)*

▶ *An early 19th century depiction of the so-called 'Black Hole' of Calcutta. While early British historians took this incident as an atrocity at the hands of Siraj, it appears that the Nawab was unaware of the awful conditions to which his English captives were subjected in Fort William. Nonetheless, for countless generations, the Black Hole was seen as the primary reason for Clive's actions which ended at Plassey. (Anne S. K. Brown Military Collection, Brown University Library)*

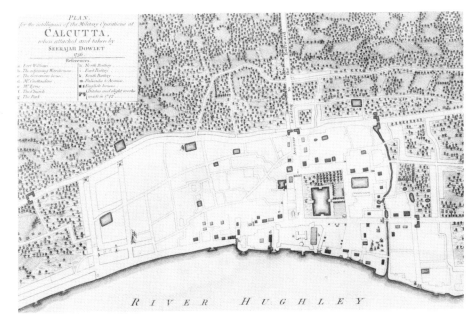

The Recapture of Calcutta

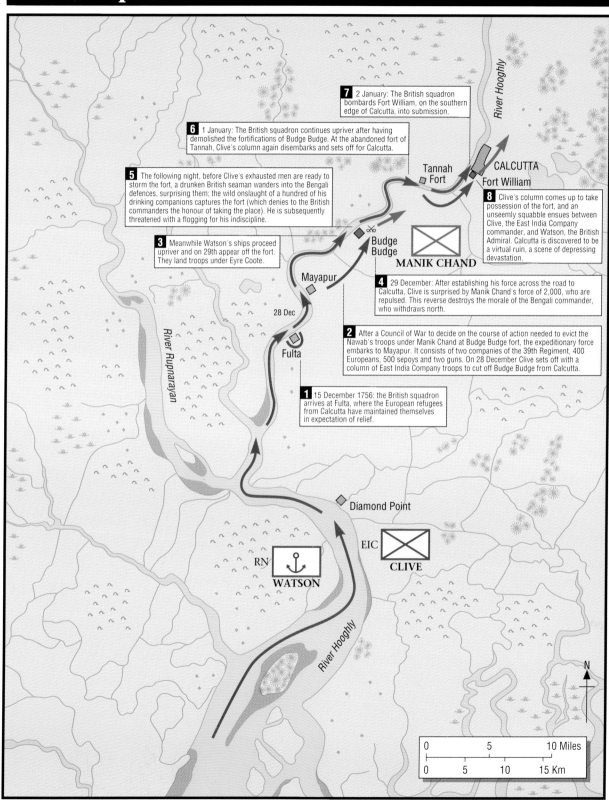

7 2 January: The British squadron bombards Fort William, on the southern edge of Calcutta, into submission.

6 1 January: The British squadron continues upriver after having demolished the fortifications of Budge Budge. At the abandoned fort of Tannah, Clive's column again disembarks and sets off for Calcutta.

5 The following night, before Clive's exhausted men are ready to storm the fort, a drunken British seaman wanders into the Bengali defences, surprising them; the wild onslaught of a hundred of his drinking companions captures the fort (which denies to the British commanders the honour of taking the place). He is subsequently threatened with a flogging for his indiscipline.

3 Meanwhile Watson's ships proceed upriver and on 29th appear off the fort. They land troops under Eyre Coote.

8 Clive's column comes up to take possession of the fort, and an unseemly squabble ensues between Clive, the East India Company commander, and Watson, the British Admiral. Calcutta is discovered to be a virtual ruin, a scene of depressing devastation.

4 29 December: After establishing his force across the road to Calcutta, Clive is surprised by Manik Chand's force of 2,000, who are repulsed. This reverse destroys the morale of the Bengali commander, who withdraws north.

2 After a Council of War to decide on the course of action needed to evict the Nawab's troops under Manik Chand at Budge Budge fort, the expeditionary force embarks to Mayapur. It consists of two companies of the 39th Regiment, 400 Europeans, 500 sepoys and two guns. On 28 December Clive sets off with a column of East India Company troops to cut off Budge Budge from Calcutta.

1 15 December 1756: the British squadron arrives at Fulta, where the European refugees from Calcutta have maintained themselves in expectation of relief.

River Hooghly

Tannah Fort

CALCUTTA
Fort William

Budge Budge

MANIK CHAND

Mayapur

28 Dec

Fulta

River Rupnarayan

Diamond Point

RN
WATSON

EIC
CLIVE

River Hooghly

N

0		5		10 Miles
0	5		10	15 Km

forts. The Nawab immediately ordered this to stop. While the French complied, the British refused, saying it was their right to fortify Calcutta. This was the opportunity he had been waiting for. With a large force, Siraj surrounded the factory at Cossimbazar near Murshidabad and arrested several British officials, including William Watts and the young Warren Hastings, before moving on to Calcutta.

The Black Hole

Panic spread through the European and Indian communities around the city as everyone including the governor, Roger Drake, made their way to safety abroad ships on the River Hooghly, while 150 men, women and children were left behind in Fort William. The city of Calcutta was occupied on 16 June by Siraj's men without a struggle and after a brief two-day siege, the fort surrendered. The leader of the garrison, John Zephaniah Holwell, tried to organize a proper surrender, but the Indians quickly overran the fort. Holwell was taken to the Nawab, who informed him that the English prisoners had nothing to fear. However, as no suitable accommodation could be found, a number of prisoners estimated at between 39 and 69 in number were herded into a small prison in Fort William measuring twenty feet by twenty feet – known as a 'black hole' in the military parlance of the day for a cell in a military barracks. On the night of 20 June 1756, between 18 and 43 persons died from asphixiation or heat exhaustion while others went delirious. Further details of the tragedy are vague or have been elaborated over time; indeed some commentators have dismissed it as pure propaganda. Whatever the situation, it appears that Siraj was unaware of the fate of his captives, and it was probably due to a mistake on the part of one of the Nawab's officers who may have been unaware of the close confines of the room. What is now apparent is that it was not a *deliberate* atrocity.

When the news broke in Madras on 16 August that Calcutta had fallen, the Council in the town summoned Clive from Fort St. David. The governor, George Pigot, was in favour of immediate action to recover the city, and Clive was in agreement. The command of the land forces of this expedition was awarded to him, and he quickly set about making the necessary arrangements before embarking on 16 October with 600 Europeans, three companies of Royal troops and over 900 sepoys. The voyage took more than six weeks, and it was not until December that they entered the Hooghly river, having made contact with the English evacuees from Calcutta and taking the fort at Budge Budge from the Nawab's garrison there. By dawn on 2 January 1757, Calcutta was finally sighted. The force was landed and set out for the city while ships from the fleet headed towards Fort William, where they came under fire. Fire was returned, causing the garrison under Manik Chand to flee, while Clive's troops came up to take possession of the city.

THE BENGAL CAMPAIGN

With Calcutta retaken and the Council and Drake reinstalled there, the Company quickly set about planning a retaliatory strike against the Nawab. The town of Hooghly, twenty miles upriver, was chosen for the attack, which was to be led by Captains Eyre Coote and Kilpatrick with 650 men. These were ferried in Royal Navy ships, and after a brief bombardment the town was taken. Everything around was put to the torch in order to send a clear message to the Nawab – who, incensed, proceeded to march south with his army. Anticipating this, Clive prepared a defensive position outside Calcutta to the north-east at Barnagul having already reinforced Fort William. He also wrote to some of the leading notables in the area asking them to put pressure on the Nawab, to which they agreed.

As the Nawab moved south, however, his mood changed: he began to consider peace moves. This

◀Charles Watson, Vice Admiral of the White, in 1757. Mezzotint after a painting by Thomas Hudson. Watson led the successful attack on the fort of Gheriah in 1756 and shortly afterwards joined with Clive to recapture Calcutta from Siraj-ud-daula. (Anne S. K. Brown Military Collection, Brown University Library)

may have been a result of his concerns over his army, and he harboured doubts about the faithfulness of his great-uncle, Mir Jafar. Intimidated by what he saw of the burnt-out remains of Hooghly, he wrote immediately to Vice-Admiral Charles Watson in charge of the ships in the area offering to allow trade to continue providing Governor Drake be replaced. But as Siraj approached Calcutta his mood changed yet again, and he began to consider military conquest once more. As his vast army – estimated in the region of 40,000 infantry and cavalry – moved towards the east of the city, the Nawab was all the while writing conciliatory letters to the Europeans. His soldiers began to fire on the suburbs of the town but he missed the opportunity of cutting off the Anglo-Indian force, which Clive quickly noted. The English officer had also missed opportunities to attack the Nawab on 3 and 4 February, but at dawn on 5 February, after another attempt at negotiation had failed and with the prospect of starvation among his troops, Clive finally went on the offensive with the assistance of men from Watson's ships.

With his force of 540 European infantry and artillerymen, 600 sailors and 800 sepoys, he was able to approach the enemy camp under cover of a thick fog. They were soon discovered and received a volley of arrows and rockets, but the fog enabled them to continue to cause havoc. A charge by 300 of the Nawab's cavalry came to a disastrous end under the volley-fire of the Anglo-Indian musketry. As the fog cleared, Clive's troops realised that their situation was far from secure, for they had strayed from their intended course. The only salvation was to make for a bridge a mile further on across paddy fields. Under fire from all sides, and harrassed by horsemen, Clive managed to rally his men and make for safety across the Mahratta Ditch and into the town and fort. Total casualties were 57 killed and 137 wounded. While it was not a victory in military terms, it scared the Nawab into negotiating a treaty on 9 February 1757, promising to compensate the Company for damages suffered and to restore previous privileges. He withdrew his army to Murshidabad, concerned about another pending threat, this one from the Shah of Afghanistan who was moving towards Bengal with a large force.

While the English could now catch their breath, the threat from France was still real, and the movements of de Bussy in the Carnatic were causing some anxiety in Calcutta. A plan was developed to capture Chandernagore, a French town twenty miles north of Calcutta on the Hooghly, where the Governor, Renault, seemed to pose a threat to Bengal. However, before attacking, Clive needed to know whether the Nawab would intervene of the side of France. Again intrigue came into play. One minute Siraj was promising the help the French; the next he was shying away; and then in March 1757 William Watts was able to inform Clive that the Indian leader had consented to an attack on Chandernagore. On 8 March the Anglo-Indian force left Calcutta, followed four days later by a naval squadron under Watson. The governor was asked to surrender on the 13th and refused. The fort was well-defended, but the river passage, which was supposed to be blocked with sunken vessels, was forced by Watson's ships which began a close bombardment of the fort, suffering many casualties from musket-fire in the process. After three hours of heavy bombardment on the morning of 23 March, Renault surrendered.

Relations between the Nawab and the British had improved, but both still mistrusted the other. The unstable ruler again showed his inconstancy by attempting to block the river and prevent Watson's ships reaching Murshidabad, while he contacted de Bussy urging him on... all the while congratulating Clive on his success. The latter was aware of the Nawab's letters to the Frenchman, which served to confirm his suspicions, and he began to realise that the only hope for long-term peace was if the French were driven out of India. With this in mind, Clive and his cohorts began to manipulate the mind of the Nawab to their way of thinking. The Indian was offered compensation for debts owed by the French, and even Chandernagore, now that the fortifications had been demolished. William Watts' French opposite in the Nawab's court, Jean Law, was now dismissed and allowed to go free much to the dislike of Clive. Two weeks later, the Nawab invited him back to help him against the English.

It was around this time that Clive heard rumours from William Watts of a conspiracy at the Nawab's court to overthrow the ruler. The leading conspirators were Mir Jafar, the Nawab's uncle and paymaster of the army, Rai Durlabh, a general, and Omichand, a

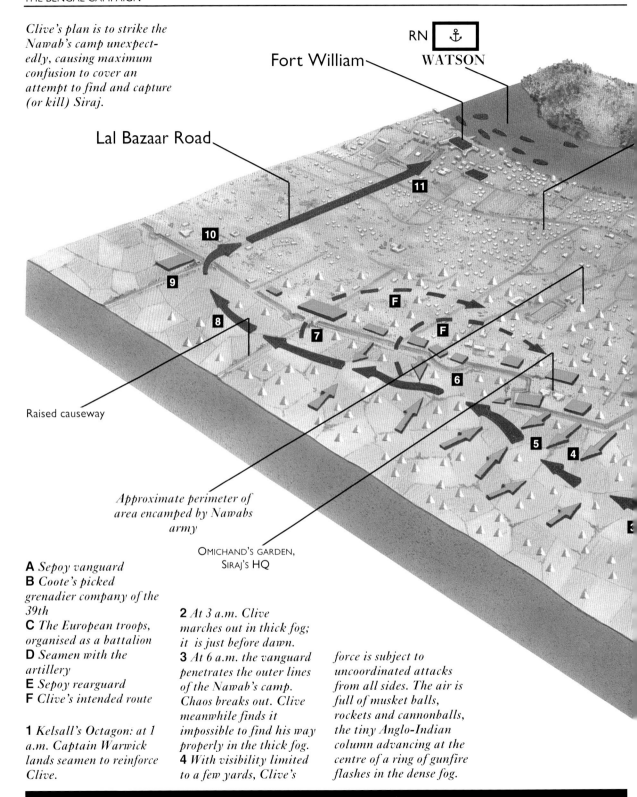

Clive's plan is to strike the Nawab's camp unexpectedly, causing maximum confusion to cover an attempt to find and capture (or kill) Siraj.

Fort William

RN ⚓
WATSON

Lal Bazaar Road

11

10

9

8

7

F

F

6

5

4

Raised causeway

Approximate perimeter of area encamped by Nawabs army

OMICHAND'S GARDEN, SIRAJ'S HQ

A Sepoy vanguard
B Coote's picked grenadier company of the 39th
C The European troops, organised as a battalion
D Seamen with the artillery
E Sepoy rearguard
F Clive's intended route

1 Kelsall's Octagon: at 1 a.m. Captain Warwick lands seamen to reinforce Clive.

2 At 3 a.m. Clive marches out in thick fog; it is just before dawn.
3 At 6 a.m. the vanguard penetrates the outer lines of the Nawab's camp. Chaos breaks out. Clive meanwhile finds it impossible to find his way properly in the thick fog.
4 With visibility limited to a few yards, Clive's

force is subject to uncoordinated attacks from all sides. The air is full of musket balls, rockets and cannonballs, the tiny Anglo-Indian column advancing at the centre of a ring of gunfire flashes in the dense fog.

RUNNING THE CALCUTTA GAUNTLET

Clive's march through the Nawab's camp, 5 February 1757

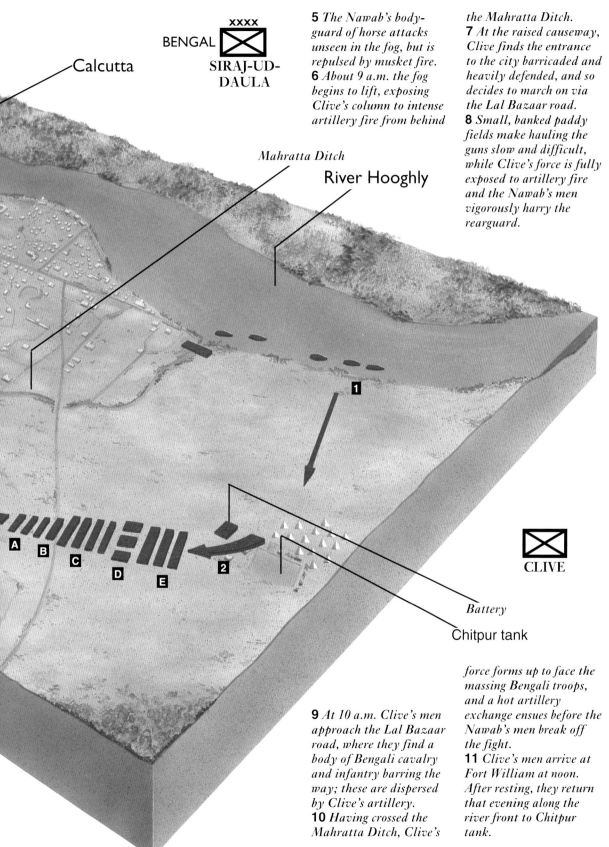

BENGAL

xxxx

SIRAJ-UD-
DAULA

Calcutta

Mahratta Ditch

River Hooghly

CLIVE

Battery

Chitpur tank

5 *The Nawab's body-guard of horse attacks unseen in the fog, but is repulsed by musket fire.*
6 *About 9 a.m. the fog begins to lift, exposing Clive's column to intense artillery fire from behind*

the Mahratta Ditch.
7 *At the raised causeway, Clive finds the entrance to the city barricaded and heavily defended, and so decides to march on via the Lal Bazaar road.*
8 *Small, banked paddy fields make hauling the guns slow and difficult, while Clive's force is fully exposed to artillery fire and the Nawab's men vigorously harry the rearguard.*

9 *At 10 a.m. Clive's men approach the Lal Bazaar road, where they find a body of Bengali cavalry and infantry barring the way; these are dispersed by Clive's artillery.*
10 *Having crossed the Mahratta Ditch, Clive's*

force forms up to face the massing Bengali troops, and a hot artillery exchange ensues before the Nawab's men break off the fight.
11 *Clive's men arrive at Fort William at noon. After resting, they return that evening along the river front to Chitpur tank.*

Sikh merchant. They were supported by an estimated four-fifths of the army. Had the Shah of Afghanistan not decided to return home, the removal of Siraj would have been complete. The Nawab himself began to hear of the rumours and removed his army to the village of Plassey as a precaution before planning to descend on Calcutta once more to remove the English threat. Clive informed Watts that he could not depend upon the friendship of Siraj and felt that his only option was to march against him in spite of one last effort at diplomacy. On 1 May, Clive and several other members of a committee decided to back the conspiracy and support Mir Jafar. A treaty between the latter and the English was drawn up while Siraj's attention was turned, and Clive agreed to have troops ready to march at twelve hours' notice to support Mir Jafar. These forces were gathered at Chandernagore although half the force was sent back to Calcutta initially.

At this point, the various conspirators began to argue among themselves over the shares that they would obtain from the overthrow of Siraj, and Omichand threatened to betray them if his share were not increased. Hearing about this, Clive suggested that two treaties be drawn-up – the one agreeing to Omichand's demands being false. While the committee reluctantly agreed to sign both, Watson refused to have anything to do with the deception and Clive was forced to forge the admiral's signature.

On 12 June 1757, word arrived that Mir Jafar had signed the treaty, and Clive began to prepare for the march. He had been sending letters of a conciliatory nature to the Nawab but now changed his tone and began threatening war. All would now rest on Mir Jafar's promise to uphold the bargain, particularly as Clive's force would be greatly outnumbered by the Nawab's.

◀ *The Bombardment of Chandernagore as depicted by Charles Dixon in 1903. Following the declaration of war, Admiral Watson saw his chance of attacking the great French settlement and fort at Chandernagore. The bombardment lasted just three hours by which time the parapets of the bastions had been almost entirely destroyed and most of the French guns dismounted. The town surrendered leaving Clive free to advance to meet the Nawab on the field of Plassey. (Anne S. K. Brown Military Collection, Brown University Library)*

THE OPPOSING COMMANDERS

Robert Clive

Clive has been accredited a great general for his victory at Plassey. Yet he was certainly far from being a military genius or for that matter, a trained soldier, although he had received some military training and did have experiences under fire prior to his great victory.

The son of an impoverished country lawyer, Clive was born at Styche Hall in the small village of Moreton Say near Market Drayton in Shropshire on 29 September 1725, the first of eleven children. As a youth, he was regarded as fiery, unruly and reckless, and on one occasion climbed the steeple of a nearby church displaying little concern for his precarious position. When he was nineteen he was nominated to be a writer in the East India Company and he set sail for Madras. The ship did not reach India until the end of 1744 following a nine-month stay in South America. His early experiences in the subcontinent led him into disciplinary problems for he exhibited a very spirited and quarrelsome nature. Frequently snubbed by his fellow workers, he led a solitary existence accompanied by fits of depression. A suicide attempt failed because the gun pointing at his head misfired twice, and he is said to have commented, 'I am reserved for something.' On another occasion he fought a duel with an officer he had accused of cheating at cards, but neither duellist came to harm.

England had been at war with France since 1744, and in 1746 the city of Madras was captured by Dupleix, Clive being among the inhabitants forced to flee to Fort St. David. It was during this period that Clive exchanged his writership for an ensign's commission in the East India Company's force. His letter of commission granted by the Governor of Fort St. David on 2 May 1747 read as follows: 'Mr. Robert Clive writer in the service being of Martial Disposition, and having acted as a Volunteer in Our Late Engagements, we have Granted him an Ensign's Commission, upon his Application for the Same.'

▼ *Stringer Lawrence, Major General and Commander-in-Chief in the East Indies. Mezzotint after painting by Sir Joshua Reynolds. Recruited by the East India Company in 1748, he led its forces against the French along the Coromandel coast. Later he helped to reorganise the Company's forces so that by the time he left India, the Company had an effective army based at Madras consisting of European companies and Indian troops. (Anne S. K. Brown Military Collection, Brown University Library)*

The French attacked Fort St. David on several occasions, which provided the young ensign with his first experience of warfare. However, the person who had perhaps the strongest influence on him was about to enter his life. In January 1748, Major Stringer Lawrence landed at the fort. Lawrence had fought at Fontenoy and Culloden and was regarded as an honest, hard-working regimental officer. He had recently been appointed commander of Fort St. George but with the capture of Madras he diverted to Fort St. David. This was a stroke of luck, for he took command of the garrison in time to repulse a final attack from the French in June 1748. Shortly afterwards, Lawrence and Clive took part in an

▶ *Robert, first Lord Clive, 1774. Steel-engraving by G. Stodart from a painting by Nathaniel Dance. In this picture, Clive wears the Order of the Bath and behind him a battle is in progress, probably intended to represent Plassey. The picture was painted four years before Clive committed suicide. (Anne S. K. Brown Military Collection, Brown University Library)*

expedition against Pondicherry led by the new com-mander of British forces in India, Admiral Edward Boscawen.

While the Treaty of Aix-la-Chapelle in 1749 brought peace, albeit short-lived, between Britain and France, there was still friction in India. During an expedition against the town of Devicotah, Clive narrowly escaped death. Now a lieutenant, he led an assault with only 35 British and 700 Indian troops. The Indians hesitated, leaving the British soldiers at the mercy of Tanjorean horseman, all but Clive and three others being killed. In the words of Lawrence, Clive 'behaved in courage and judgement much beyond what could have been expected from his years'.

Clive was involved in numerous military expedi-tions against various French and Indian forces dur-ing the Second Carnatic War between 1751 and 1753. He assisted the garrison of Trichinopoly dur-ing a siege in 1751, showed his shrewdness at Arcot and his skills of generalship at the battles of Arni and Conjeveram and returned to Madras a hero. In March 1753 the 27-year-old Clive sailed for Eng-land, where he was once again feted as a hero, this time by the directors of the East India Company. He was back in India by 1755, in time to assist Admiral

◄ The fort of Geriah from an engraving published in 1781. The British fleet under Rear-Admirals Watson and Pocock with troops under Lieutenant-Colonel Clive arrived off Geriah on 12 February 1756. The garrison, commanded by the pirate Angria, having refused to surrender, was bombarded. After three hours, many of the pirate vessels in the harbour were burning and much of the town and fort set on fire. The bombardment continued on the following day after another

refusal from the garrison to surrender. Eventually the governor showed the flag of truce and agreed to an unconditional surrender. The British force lost twenty men but the enemy suffered many casualties. Clive led his force into the town and fort on the 14th, capturing stores, 30,000 worth of valuables and £100,000 sterling. (Anne S. K. Brown Military Collection, Brown University Library)

time only for a short period. Back in England, his reputation was being tarnished by various persons in society critical of his reforms of the East India Company. Indeed, a bill 'for the better regulation of the affairs of the East India Company' was introduced in 1772. Clive accounted for his efforts in a dramatic speech to the House of Commons, which voted in May 1773 to record that Clive had 'rendered great and meritorious services to his country'. However the pressure was too much for him, and in a fit of depression he took his own life in November 1774. Clive's lasting testimony was as founder of the British Empire in India.

Siraj-ud-daula

In contrast to Clive, very little is know of the Nawab of Bengal, Siraj-ud-daula. He was born in 1729 and succeeded to the Nawabship in 1756 upon the death of his grandfather, Alivardi Khan. This brought with it immense power and wealth. He also suffered from a strong inclination to alcohol, indeed an addiction, although had made a promise to his late relative that he would give it up. His loneliness in such a position brought on feelings of insecurity, which in turn generated volatile changes of mood. While prone to arrogance, he was fearful of those around him, constantly in a state of suspicion that they wanted to remove him. This applied also to Europeans, and he shared his grandfather's anxiety about the growing strength of these foreign traders at the expense of the native rulers. He mistrusted the British in particular, owing to their political intrigues with various of his relatives.

While the events surrounding the 'black hole' of Calcutta in June 1756 have painted him as a cruel and depraved despot, the truth of the matter suggests that he was unaware of the fate of the captured Europeans. None the less, numerous false stories began to surround him, such as his alleged pastime of pulling the wings off birds or watching boats deliberately overturned so that he could watch the occupants drown. In truth he was known to adore his chief wife, and his only real fault can be discerned in his weakness, which led to indecisiveness, fear and a lack of courage.

Watson in an attack upon the fort of Gheriah, home to a pirate chief named Angria who had established himself as a power in the district north of Goa. In the following year he assisted in the relief of Calcutta and in 1757 in the investment of the French town of Chandernagore.

Clive was now a powerful figure in India and began a period of political manoeuvrings with the leading Indians to gain prestige for the British over their rivals, the French. This often called for devious and ethically dubious methods to achieve results, which opened-up Clive to criticism. His participation in the plot to overthrow the Nawab, Siraj-ud-daula brought him into a questionable deal with the new claimant, Mir Jafar, whose sincerity was doubted. Believing in the latter, Clive moved against Siraj-ud-daula at Plassey and, fortunately for the general, Mir Jafar kept his promise not to use his troops in support of the Nawab, and Clive won the day.

Following Plassey, Clive was to turn his attention to the French under the Comte de Lally, who were causing difficulties for the British in Madras. Later, it would be the turn of the Dutch to be expelled. By the age of 35, Clive was immensely wealthy, and he left Calcutta for England in 1760. William Pitt called him a 'heaven-born general', while the King awarded him an Irish peerage. However, Clive was back in India by April 1765 as Governor-General and Commander-in-Chief but this

One Indian historian wrote: 'Owing to Siraj-ud-daula's harshness of temper and indulgence in vio-

▼*Portrait of Siraj-ud-daula, from a plate in Major J. H. Tull Walsh's* Murshidabad, *reproduced in S. C. Hill (ed)* Bengal in 1756–1757. *Siraj-ud-daula is somewhat of an enigma due to the dearth of details*

about him. What is known is that he was strongly suspicious of everyone around him, fearful that they were out to kill him. He was also naïve in his trust of several of his generals. This led to his defeat at

Plassey and eventual murder. (Anne S. K. Brown Military Collection, Brown University Library)

▼*Much of Moghul court life took place out of doors or in tented enclosures. It remained as splendid as ever even as Moghul power declined. The horseman from Hyderabad appears to be bringing bad news*

lent language, fear and terror had settled on the hearts of everyone to such an extent that no one among his generals of the army or the noblemen of the city was free from anxiety... Siraj-ud-daula treated all the noblemen and generals... with ridicule and drollery, and bestowed on each some contemptuous nickname that ill-suited any of them.' Others have written that Siraj displayed facets of a character common to oriental dynastic politics of the period.

In terms of his military prowess, his successes on the field of battle should be attributed more to his military advisers than to any inherent skills of his own. He also had the benefit of a large army, which outnumbered the majority of European armies then in the subcontinent. Indeed, had Mir Jafar and others joined the Nawab in the action at Plassey rather than staying inactive, the battle might have been only a footnote in Anglo-Indian military history.

Shortly after Plassey, Siraj met his death at the hands of conspirators in Murshidabad.

THE OPPOSING ARMIES

The Army of the East India Company

The small Anglo-Indian force that faced the hordes of soldiers from the Nawab's army on the morning of 23 June 1757 across a small pasture near the hamlet of Plassey was hardly an army in the true sense; it was a mixed group of British soldiers, native sepoys and topasses, or Indo-Portuguese soldiers. There are few details concerning this force, and what little is known has been gleaned from a handful of sources. In all, Clive had approximately 1,000 European troops and 2,000 sepoys commanded by English officers, with eight 6-pounder guns and two howitzers. The force consisted of detachments of the Bengal, Madras and Bombay artillery, the British 39th Regiment, and the Bengal, Madras and Bombay European Regiments. Serving with the artillery were some fifty sailors from the fleet, and there were some companies of Bengal and Madras sepoys.

Royal Regiments

Four regiments were awarded a battle honour for Plassey: the 39th Regiment of Foot, and three regiments of the East India Company, the Bengal European Regiment, the 1st Madras European Regiment, and the Bombay European Regiment.

By 1754, the increasing difficulties faced by the East India Company in protecting its interests resulted in an appeal for London to dispatch a Royal regiment. The dispatch of the 39th, with a detachment of Royal Artillery, was the response. Under the command of Colonel John Aldercron, the regiment followed the standard set down under the British establishment of 3 sergeants, 3 corporals, 2 drummers and 70 privates for each company, with a quartermaster and a surgeon's mate. As there was little time for recruiting, the regiment drafted men from other units. A number of officers refused to go out to India and took retirement, and these were largely replaced by younger, inexperienced men.

ORDER OF BATTLE, THE ANGLO-INDIAN ARMY (EAST INDIA COMPANY) AT PLASSEY

Commander-in-Chief: Robert Clive
Strength: circa 3,000 men

Advanced Detachment
Two 6-pounders, two howitzers

LEFT WING	CENTRE	RIGHT WING
Native Troops	European Troops:	Native Troops

1st Division	**3rd Division**
(Madras Regiment)	HM 39th Regiment
Major Kilpatrick	Major Coote

2nd Division	**4th Division**
(Madras & Bombay Regiments)	(Bombay Europeans)
Major Grant	Major Guah (or Gaupp)

▶*1st Bengal European Regiment, 1760. Watercolour by Harry Payne. The European regiments of Bengal, Bombay and Madras wore general issue clothing of red tunics, black hats and white gaiters. They were manned by British soldiers. (Anne S. K. Brown Military Collection, Brown University Library)*

Two additional companies raised in the Midlands arrived in India in 1756, one of which was commanded by Lieutenant Eyre Coote. Once in India, the transportation of the regiment required 8 tumbrils, 6 for ammunition, 1 for medicines and 1 to

◀ *Reconstruction of a sepoy of the 1st Battalion Bengal Native Infantry at Plassey in 1757. Water-colour by Frederick Todd. There are few details of the clothing worn by sepoys of this period and this reconstruction is somewhat conjectural. (Anne S. K. Brown Military Collection, Brown University Library)*

▶ *Sepoys of the 3rd Battalion at Bombay. Engraving published in London by M. Darly in 1773. The native battalions were raised by Clive to compensate for the shortage of European troops. Three battalions were raised and uniformed along European lines. Sepoys served with distinction in the three Presidency armies from their origins in the 18th century and continued to do so under the Crown following the 1857 uprising. (Anne S. K. Brown Military Collection, Brown University Library)*

carry the money chest, pulled by a total of 48 draft and 84 carriage bullocks including 11 for the field officers and captains, 1 each for the surgeon and his mates, and the quartermaster, and 10 for the 20 sub-alterns. The adjutant travelled by horse, while the colonel had the luxury of a palanquin, a box-like structure carried by natives.

Just two months before the Battle of Plassey, the roll call of the 39th Regiment in camp near Chinsura was: three captains, four lieutenants, five ensigns, eight sergeants, ten corporals, seven drummers and 213 privates. At the battle the regiment lost no men, but a sergeant and three privates were wounded.

There having been little thought given to adjusting military dress for tropical wear, the men wore the uniforms they had been issued in Britain, which were based on the regulation 1751 uniform. This consisted of a thick wool coat of scarlet, faced with pale green lapels and cuffs, and bearing white lace, with scarlet waistcoats and breeches, white gaiters (brown for marching) and buff belts, plus a black cocked hat bound with white lace. The musicians carried drums painted with '39' on them, while the green regimental colour had the Union

flag in the upper left and the numerals 'XXXIX' surrounded by a wreath of laurels. In 1760 the regiment is reported as having '630 iron-hilted swords and 70 iron-hilted scimitars'. The main firearm was the East India flintlock musket, a weapon of some 46 inches in length derived from the Brown Bess.

The 1st Madras European Regiment was the second body of troops established by the East India Company in the 1660s but was not formed into a battalion until 1748. Its first colonel was Stringer Lawrence, who arrived at Fort St. David in January 1748 with a commission to command the Company's forces in India. From then on, the Madras European Regiment saw action throughout the various conflicts with the French in India. According to the roll taken in the camp near Chinsura on 7 April 1757, the Madras regiment numbered 1 major, 5 captains, 5 lieutenants, 4 ensigns, 5 volunteers, 41 sergeants, 26 corporals, 10 drummers and 105 privates. The officers were Major Kilpatrick; Captains Lin, Maskelyne, Callender, Gaupp, with Captains Rumbold, Wagner and Fischer as supernumeries and Fraser as Adjutant; Lieutenants Campbell, who served as quartermaster, Knox, Tuite, Scotney and Joecher; and Ensigns Tabby, Oswald and Wiecks. The regiment lost 1 killed and 3 wounded at Plassey.

Of the Royal Artillery detachment, little is known. It appears that the artillery companies serving in India in 1756 and 1757 were those of Northall, Hislop and Maitland. Maitland's and Northall's companies saw action at Gheriah fort in 1756. Captain William Hislop's detachment was at Fort St. George between January and May of 1757 and in camp at Chingleput in June. In January of 1757, Hislop's detachment consisted of 6 officers, 1 cadet, 2 sergeants, 2 corporals, 5 bombardiers, 20 gunners, 9 mattrosses and 1 drummer. It is known that at Plassey, there were 171 artillerymen, includ-

◀*Sepoy Officer, 1757. Watercolour by Charles Lyall. The clothing of the sepoy troops who served with Clive at Plassey is not described in any of the contemporary accounts. As a conse-* *quence, many of the illustrations are based more on guesswork than anything else. (Anne S. K. Brown Military Collection, Brown University Library)*

ing 50 sailors and 7 midshipmen, with 10 field pieces and 2 small howitzers, commanded by Lieutenant Hater of the Royal Navy.

The artillery had been serving with the Company for several years and supplied materials for various expeditions. For instance, a list compiled by Capt.-Lt. Joseph Winter of the Royal Artillery in February 1756 recorded that Coehorn mortars, shells for 10-inch guns and mortars, corned powder, stools for drawing knives, a laboratory chest, and sponges, were issued to three naval vessels for the attack on Gheriah. Additional items were issued to a Bomb Battery and to a lieutenant. The artillerymen were paid with a gold coin known as a Pagoda,

▶*Indian Armour in a lithograph from a picture drawn from nature by Captain John Luard, c. 1840. According to Luard, armour was principally worn by the cavalry which had always been the major strength of native Indian armies. The picture was made from armour captured when the fort of Bhurtpore was captured in 1826. (Anne S. K. Brown Military Collection, Brown University Library)*

which was worth about 8s. a coin. In 1762, artillery officers were paid as follows: major 5s., adjutant 6s., quartermaster 4s., surgeon 6s, and the commissary and paymaster 8s. In 1762 an artillery company serving with the East India Company in Madras mustered 3 sergeants, 3 corporals and 8 bombardiers, 20 gunners and 42 mattrosses, 2 drummers and 1 fifer.

Native Troops

Faced in early 1757 with a shortage of men to confront the dual threat from the force of the Nawab and the French settlers of Chandernagore, Clive reorganised the Bengal troops under his command into regular battalions officered by a small British contingent. Prior to this, native troops (called Buxarries in Bengal, and Telingas or Peons in Madras) had been employed when the need arose; these had been wholly undisciplined and were armed and equipped in native style. Even the better trained sepoys from Madras and Bombay still wore native dress and used native equipment.

Recruiting for the first native battalion was quite easy. Large numbers of fighting men had been forced down into the lower provinces in search of service by the general disturbances in the governments of northern India and the incursions of Muslims into Bengal. The body of troops raised around Calcutta included Pathans, Jats, Rajputs and Rohillas. Another battalion was raised in Calcutta in August 1757, and subsequent battalions followed. Clive wanted to assimilate them as near as possible to European troops. The three or four hundred picked men were organised into three new units, armed and dressed along European lines. They were drilled and disciplined as regular troops, and Clive appointed a British officer and non-commissioned officers to command and instruct them. This Bengal native regiment was for many years known as Lal Paltan on account of its equipment and later it became known as Gillis-ki-paltan, a name derived

▶ *Indian armour in the Museo Stibbert, Florence. The right-hand figure wears a garment of soft red cloth to which small pieces of brass armour* *etched with gold are fastened. (Anne S. K. Brown Military Collection, Brown University Library)*

A Deccani native gouache painting of Daleel Khan, a celebrated general under the Emperor Abdullah, c. 1750. The figure wears elaborate clothing and his weaponry includes a spear, shield, curved sword and bow and arrows. Little is known about this general but his clothing is not unlike that worn by some of Siraj-ud-daula's officers at Plassey. (Anne S. K. Brown Military Collection, Brown University Library)

▶A native gouache painting dating from 1751 representing the Maharajah Sree Bukht Sing Jee of Jodhpur. This well-armed figure wears a long coat and leggings of mail and a steel helmet. His horse also has a protective face guard of mail. This clothing is typical of Indian martial costume of the 1750s. (Anne S. K. Brown Military Collection, Brown University Library)

from Captain Primrose Galliez, who commanded the regiment in 1763. In 1796 it became the 2nd Battalion of the 12th Bengal Native Infantry.

Information on the early uniforms of native enlisted men is scarce. Red cloth was supplied, and the coat followed roughly the cut of the British model, but the overall garb reflected a native flavour. All these troops were infantry, and there do not appear to have been native cavalry in any of the three presidencies.

Other native soldiers came from the town of Baksar in Bihar, whose men had a long history of serving as foot soldiers in various Muslim armies. At Plassey they served as gunners and matchlock-men.

The Army of the Nawab of Bengal

There are few surviving details concerning the army Siraj-ud-daula commanded. At Plassey there were about 35,000 untrained and undisciplined soldiers. Colonel G. B. Malleson writing in 1885 described them as 'men not trained in the European fashion but of the stamp of those which may be seen in the present day in and about the chief towns of the territories of native princes of the second or third rank. They were, in fact, men imperfectly trained and imperfectly armed, and, in the rigid sense of the word, undisciplined.' They were armed with matchlocks, pikes, swords, bows and arrows. The Nawab also had the use of 15,000 cavalry who were somewhat better organised. These were mostly Pathan tribesmen armed with swords and long spears, and riding large horses. The clothing worn by the Nawab's men was as diverse as their ethnic origins. It is known that some men, probably cavalry, wore armour of mail manufactured in Lahore. Such armour consisted of a *zirih* or coat, trousers of mail, a *khud* or helmet, and a rectangular breast plate called a *chaharainah*.

The French Artillery Contingent

The Company of the Indies (*La Compagnie des Indes*) was authorised by Royal decree in 1721 for service in India and Africa. Throughout the 1740s and 1750s the French East India Company employed these troops effectively in India at numerous battles against both the Indians and the British and a number served under the Marquis de Bussy between 1751 and 1754. These were mainly volunteer companies under the command of de Bussy himself, M. de Kerjean, a nephew of Dupleix, and M. de Vincent. On 15 January 1751, the role call of the French East India Company's troops at Pondicherry numbered 300 Europeans, 100 native sepoys (*cipaye*) and topasses (*topas*) six artillery pieces of 2 and 3 calibre, 2 bronze mortars and 8 munition wagons. In 1756, the entire total of the

ORDER OF BATTLE, THE BENGAL ARMY

Commander-in-Chief: Siraj-ud-daula

STRENGTH: about 33–40,000 Bengali infantry
plus about 18,000 Pathan cavalry

ARTILLERY: 50 guns, mainly 24pdrs and 32pdrs, with
detachment of 4 guns under St. Frais (50 Frenchmen)

Advanced Cavalry
Mir Madan and Mohan Lal

Left Wing	Centre	Right Wing
Mir Jafar	Yar Lutuf Khan	Rai Durlabh

Compagnie des Indes numbered around 6,000 men and 250 officers.

At Plassey, however, the only French troops present were 50 artillerymen who had escaped from the garrison at Chandernagore under the command of Monsieur St. Frais (or Sinfray), formerly of the Council of Chandranagar. They were in charge of an impressive artillery train of 53 large guns, mainly 18-, 24- and 32-pounders. Having suffered at the hands of the British, they were eager for revenge. This small French contingent also had four of its own guns.

Each Indian gun with its carriage and tumbril was mounted on a large wooden platform about six feet from the ground moved by wheels, the whole drawn by forty or fifty white bullocks. Behind each gun was an elephant trained to use its head to push when required. The Indian force also had a considerable number of rockets. The Nawab's army included elephants covered with chain mail and plate armour. These animals had been used in Muslim armies for centuries, initially in an aggressive role but more and more they became beasts of burden. While there are no written accounts of the use of elephants at Plassey, a contemporary hand-coloured drawing depicts several elephants in action, one of which has been shot down. A note below the drawing reads: 'The English troops had no sooner begun to fire when the Nabob's Army retired... by which many of the Nabob's men were killed and wounded and some of the Elephants.' In his report of the battle to the Committee at Fort William, Clive states that three elephants were killed. In the Royal Armouries, at the Tower of London, is a model of an elephant covered with original mail said to have been collected by Clive at Plassey.

▲ *Reconstruction of a North Indian silladar horseman of the 18th century, based upon a suit of armour in the Tower of London and other sources. Watercolour by Frederick Todd. (Anne S. K. Brown* *Military Collection, Brown University Library)*

PL. V

▲ *A volunteer in the army of the Marquis de Bussy during the campaign in the Deccan region of India, 1756, from a picture by Lucien Rousselot. The figure wears a navy blue coat with red facings, white leggings and a bearskin-covered grenadier cap. It is doubtful if these troops managed to retain such a smart appearance while toiling in the miserable climate experienced in the subcontinent. (Anne S. K. Brown Military Collection, Brown University Library)*

▲ *A modern representation of French soldiers serving in India in the 1750s from a picture by Lucien Rousselot in* Le Passepoil. *On the left is a soldier of Kerjean's company, 1751, while on the right stand an artilleryman and a dragoon of Bussy's force in 1753. The figure on the left wears a red coat with green facings while those on the right are dressed in green coats and red facings. (Anne S. K. Brown Military Collection, Brown University Library)*

◀ *A French soldier of Kerjean's company in India, 1760, from a watercolour painted in 1866. The figure wears a uniform designed by their colonel consisting of a red tunic faced with green, white waistcoat breeches and gaiters. The collar is brown and the hat has gold embroidery on it with a white plume. (Anne S. K. Brown Military Collection, Brown University Library)*

▶ *A cipaye (sepoy) serving in Dupleix's army in India in 1756 from a picture by Lucien Rousselot. While there were no French sepoys present at the battle of Plassey, the French made good use of native troops during their campaigns in India in the 1740s and 50s. French cipayes wore a uniform consisting of a white jacket and a type of skirt with a flat hat. (Anne S. K. Brown Military Collection, Brown University Library)*

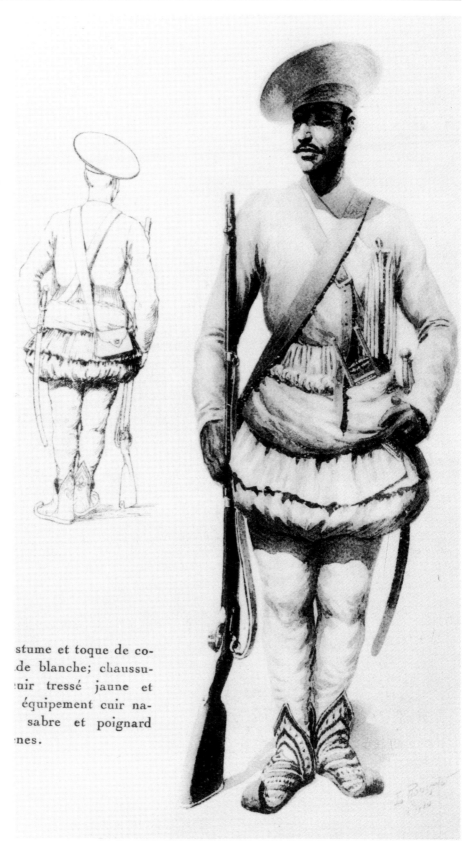

stume et toque de co-
de blanche; chaussu-
uir tressé jaune et
équipement cuir na-
sabre et poignard
nes.

PLASSEY:
THE APPROACH MARCH

On 12 June, Clive was joined by Kilpatrick and the rest of the army from Calcutta at Chandernagore, and on the following day the captured fort was turned over to Lieutenant Clarke, who occupied it with 100 sailors. The Anglo-Indian force consisted of 613 european troops and 171 artillerymen controlling ten field guns.; the native contingent was composed of 91 topasses and 2,100 sepoys. An additional 150 sailors from Watson's fleet completed the force on the understanding that they were to serve as soldiers and not porters. Everything was now set for the column to march, which it did on the 13th. In fact, only the Indian troops actually marched, as the Europeans moved up the Hooghly river in boats. Having traversed a level country only occasionally broken by palms, hardwoods and some jungle, and passing via the Dutch settlement at Cinsura, the force found itself twenty miles north of the town of Hooghly on the 14th. On the same day, Watts and his companions met up with Clive's force and informed the general that the conspiracy was gaining momentum and that many were flocking to Mir Jafar's side. At this point, Clive sent a declaration of war to the Nawab. By the 16th, the force had reached Paltee.

Just over twelve miles farther north lay the strategic town of Katwa, situated overlooking the road and the river. There was known to be a large supply of rice in the fort there, which would be an important supply for the army, and Clive therefore ordered Coote to take a detachment and capture the fort. The major took 200 Europeans, 500 sepoys, a 6-pounder and a howitzer and arrived about 10 p.m. three miles south of the town. Two hours later, Coote captured some prisoners who informed him that the garrison of 2,000 men in Katwa had retired into the fort half a mile away, and that 10,000 horsemen under Raja Manik Chand, former governor of Calcutta, were expected to reinforce the town shortly. Coote's

small force was discovered when one of his men was suddenly taken ill and in a delirious state made noise sufficient to alert the garrison. Firing continued at daybreak on the 19th, forcing Coote to alter his plans. He sent in a flag of truce, and the governor of the fort was informed that Coote's force was there to assist them against the Nawab: that the fort should therefore be surrendered. This ploy was rejected. Coote decided to split his Anglo-Indian force, one group crossing the river to open a heavy fire on the fort while the other crossed farther up. When the force advanced towards the fort, the enemy gave up and fled.

Informed of the success, Clive arrived in person at 2 p.m. with the bulk of the army reaching Katwa at midnight – just before monsoon rains hit the town, forcing the soldiers to quit their tents and find drier shelter in the huts within the place. The town was supposed to be the rendezvous for Clive and Mir Jafar, but the latter failed to arrive, and his letter explaining his absence did not reach the British camp until after Plassey. In fact, Mir Jafar had by now been approached by the Nawab to seek reconciliation. The Nawab was aware of the advancing force and was hindered by the defection of many of his supporters and was not confident of the support he could expect to receive from the small French contingent. Mir Jafar concluded an agreement of sorts with his foe and attempted to inform Clive that he himself planned to abide by the treaty. However, Clive had received intelligence to the contrary suggesting that his agreement with Mir Jafar was now void.

Clive was faced with a dilemma. If he no longer had the support of Mir Jafar, it would be suicidal to confront the the Nawab's large army. He decided to confer with his staff about the best approach and informed them that Mir Jafar could not now by relied upon. He also wrote to the Council in Calcutta to invite their suggestions.

▶ *Eyre Coote*
(1726–1783), as depicted
in an engraving by
Walker, was perhaps the
best know of Clive's offi-
cers at Plassey. He first
saw India as a young offi-
cer of the 39th Regiment
in 1754 and his first action
was in the relief of Cal-
cutta. His success at
Katwa during the
approach march to
Plassey enabled Clive to
consolidate his force and
provide the momentum
needed to take on the
much larger army of the
Nawab. Some years after
the battle he returned to
England but was back in
the subcontinent as
colonel of the 84th Regi-
ment shortly afterwards,
and he served with dis-
tinction in the campaigns
against the French under
Lally at Wandiwash and
Pondicherry. A brief
respite in England in the
early 1760s, when he
served as a member of par-
liament, was followed by
another term in India
starting in 1778. This
final period was to see him
in action against Hyder
Ali before his health
failed him in 1781 and he
relinquished his com-
mand. (Anne S. K. Brown
Military Collection,
Brown University
Library)

On 21 June 1757, Clive held a council of war at Cuttawa.* He put the following question to his officers: 'Whether in our present situation without assistance and on our own bottom it would be pru-dent to attack the Nabob, or whether we should wait till joined by some Country Power.' Thirteen officers including Clive were against immediate action, while the minority including Coote reasoned that as they had achieved considerable success already with little opposition, any delay might dampen the already high spirits of the men. The distance from Calcutta also demanded some swift action before the whole force ran out of supplies.

Shortly after the council of war broke up, Clive

* With Colonel Clive, President, were present: Major Kilpatrick, Captains Gaupp, Rumbold, Campbell, and Capt.-Lieut. Passhaud of the Madras army; Majors Archibald Grant and Coote, Captains Waggoner and Corneille of the 39th; Captains Alexander Grant, Cudmore, Fisher, Muir, Le Beaume, and Casters of the Bengal contingent; Captains Palmer and Armstrong, and Captain-Lieut. Molitaire of Bombay; and Jennings of the artillery. Captain Hater, lieutentant of the Royal Navy, did not give his opinion because he considered that he did not have a proper seat on the council.

▶*Indian miniature portrait of Mir Jafar as Nawab of Bengal, by a Murshidabad artist. Had it not been for Mir Jafar's treachery towards his master, Siraj-ud-daula, Clive's moment of victory would have been a catastrophic defeat and possibly the end of British supremacy in the subcontinent. But Jafar's inactivity at Plassey allowed Clive to concentrate his efforts upon the main part of the Bengali army within the entrenchment. (The British Library)*

approached Coote informing him that, despite the majority vote *against* action, the army was to march next morning, and informed the men to stand ready. Unknown to Clive, the Committee in Calcutta had replied to his letter by urging the general to move to battle, but this was not received until after the victory. At 6 o'clock on the morning of 22 June 1757, the small Anglo-Indian force crossed the River Baggiruttee and marched two miles in pouring rain, then rested upon soggy ground before resuming their march, reaching their destination at one in the morning beyond the small village of Plassey (or *Palasi*). They established a position in an orchard of mango trees about 800 yards long and 300 yards wide called Laksha Bagh which formed a grove, the area being enclosed by a ditch and mud wall stretching 300 yards adjacent to a hunting lodge formally owned by the Nawab.

Siraj had been at his fortified camp at Plassey twenty miles south of Murshidabad for several days. Since March, there had been about 2,000 men in this camp under Rai Durlabh, but this number had swelled throughout May and June. The Nawab hoped that a French force under Jean Law would be able to join him, but this was not to be. Indeed, the Nawab had offered money to Law to return to Murshidabad, but the Frenchman refused. This was a setback for the Nawab. Even though he commanded a strategically strong position, he had little faith in his soldiers, many of whom he suspected of being involved in the conspiracy – he knew that many of his generals were and that their supporters were only present because of cash inducements.

The Nawab's position lay behind earthen entrenchments running at right-angles to the river and then forming a three-mile line running in a north-easterly direction. Just in from the river along

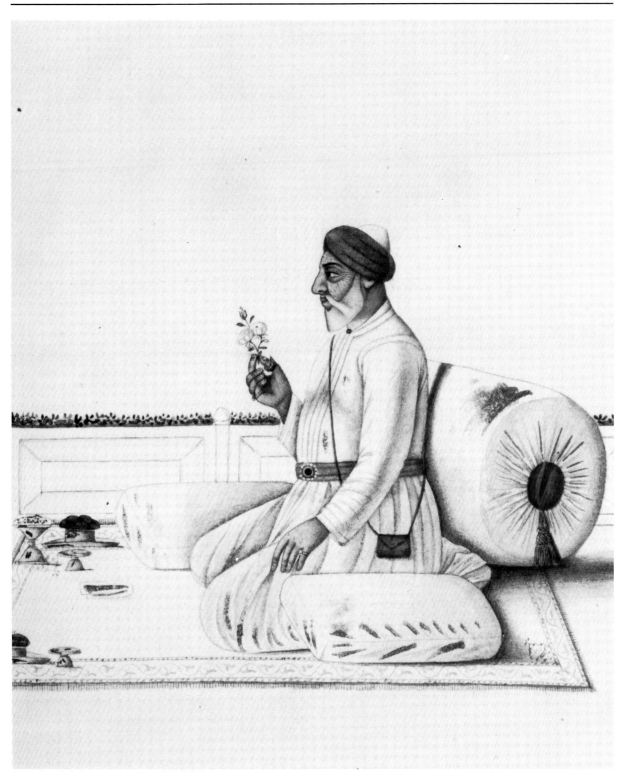

the entrenchment was a redoubt defended by cannon; and situated three hundred yards east of this was a small hill, densely covered with trees. Eight hundred yards farther on towards the British position in the grove was a small tank or artificial lake and a larger one lay 100 yards beyond. The earth that had been removed to create these artificial basins surrounded them.

THE BATTLE OF PLASSEY

As the mist rolled across the plain at break of day on 23 June while black monsoon clouds hung overhead, the army of Siraj-ud-daula began to move towards the mango grove where the Anglo-Indian force was entrenched. The whole plain was covered with the Nawab's men, horses, elephants and bullocks, presenting as one Englishman observed, 'a most pompous and formidable appearance'. Orme estimated that the Bengali army, marching in separate and compact bodies, numbered 50,000 (a more realistic number would be 35,000 to 40,000 infantry) armed mainly with matchlocks, but carrying pikes, swords, arrows and rockets. There were 18,000 Pathans, mounted troops from northern India. 50 cannon, mostly 24- and 32-pounders, were mounted on large platforms. Orme describes these as follows: 'A large stage, raised six feet from the ground, carrying besides the cannon, all the ammunition belonging to it, and the gunners themselves who managed the cannon, on the stage itself. These machines were drawn by 40 or 50 yoke of white oxen, of the largest size, bred in the country of Purnea; and behind each cannon walked an elephant, trained to assist at difficult tugs, by shoving with his forehead against the hinder part of the carriage.' Some of these elephants were covered in metal armour. A small group of about 50 Frenchman under the command of M. de St. Frais (Sinfray) moved towards the tank nearest the grove, about half a mile from it, with four small light can-

▶ *The Nawab's artillery on its movable platform from a drawing by Richard Caton Woodville for the* Illustrated London News, *1893. A unusual feature connected with Siraj-ud-daula's artillery was that the guns were mounted on great platforms built on wheels and hauled by fifty yoke of oxen and elephants. (Anne S. K. Brown Military Collection, Brown University Library)*

non, while two larger guns under the command of a native officer were positioned in line with the tank near the bend of the river. Part of Siraj's force of 5,000 horse and 7,000 infantry under the his one faithful general, Mir Madan, and Siraj's favourite, Mohan Lal, took up a position between the tank and the river. The remaining part of the force com-

manded by the confederates to the plot, Mir Jafar on the left near the British, Yar Lutuf Khan in the centre and Rai Durlabh on the right, extended from Mir Madan's left in large columns in a curve from a hill covered with jungle near their camp to the east of the southern angle of the grove towards the village of Plassey, about 800 yards from the British

position, threatening to enclose Clive's small army in its forward sweep. Field pieces were interspersed between the columns along with dense masses of infantry and mounted troops. One estimate puts the number of troops in this curve at 45,000, and it was regarded as a very strong position. An attack by the Anglo-Indian force on the position occupied by the French and Mir Madan would expose their right to a flank attack.

Clive himself moved to the roof-top of the hunting lodge to observe the unfolding situation and to await any further developments from Mir Jafar. He was depressed at having not heard from Mir Jafar, but, observing the vast host arrayed

▲ A view of a water tank as depicted by Captain Charles Gold of the Royal Artillery in the 1790s. In order to keep the land suitable for cultiva- *tion, many tanks or reservoirs were built to catch the rain from the monsoons. These structures were well embanked with earth. At Plassey, two*

before him, he commented: 'We must make the best fight we can during the day and at night sling our muskets over our shoulders and march back to Calcutta.' He was surprised and impressed at the size and splendour of the Nawab's army and quickly came to the realisation that his position was not only flanked but that his rear was threatened by the end of the curve. Doubts must have crossed his mind as

tanks surrounded by earth situated in the middle of the battlefield formed strong points d'appui for the Nawab, and a redoubt armed with cannon further strengthened the Bengali position. (Anne S. K. Brown Military Collection)

▶Right: The arrival of Siraj at Plassey from a drawing by Richard Caton Woodville for the Illustrated London News, 1893. This is a purely imaginary scene, typical of the Victorian illustrated press, although the Nawab no doubt travelled in a howdah on the back of an elephant. The origin of the design of the flag born by the mounted standard bearer is unknown. (Anne S. K. Brown Military Collection, Brown University Library)

to whether all the troops arrayed before him would be faithful to the Nawab. If they were, his fate and those of his men would be sealed.

At seven o'clock in the morning, he sent Mir Jafar the following short message: 'Whatever could be done by me I have done, I can do no more. If you will come to Daudipore I will march from Placis [*sic*] to meet you, but if you won't comply even this, pardon me, I shall make it up with the Nabob.' He had considered several alternatives to a battle, one of which was to make peace with the Nawab if the latter's force seemed too great, but the battle broke out before the general could make such a move.

Resolved to meet his foe, Clive ordered his men out of the grove and to form into line. He could muster only about 900 European troops including 100 artillerists and 50 sailors, 100 topasses and 2,100 sepoys. These troops were moved from their night position to a line stretching from the river on the west to the outer edge of the grove to the east. He had only eight 6-pounders and two howitzers (Coote, however, mentions only one); the 6-pounders were arrayed in groups of three on each side of the battalion of European troops, who were stationed in four divisions in the centre flanked on the right and left by two divisions of sepoys. The first division under Major Kilpatrick was composed of the Madras Regiment; the second, under Major Grant consisted of troops from both the Madras

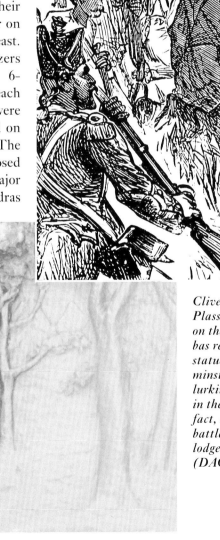

Clive at the Battle of Plassey. The illustration on the left is one of the bas relief panels on the statue to Clive in Westminster, and depicts him lurking (strangely alone) in the mango grove. In fact, he spent much of the battle atop the hunting lodge and then inside it. (DAG)

and Bengal Regiments; the third under Major Coote consisted of the 39th (or Aldercron's) Regiment; and the final division was made up of of the Bombay Europeans under Major Guah (or Gaupp). Ahead of the left wing of sepoys closest to the river were two brick-kilns, and Clive ordered that the two remaining guns and the howitzers be deployed here, about 200 yards from his position, to check the fire of the French.

The Battle Begins

At eight o'clock, the French contingent under M. de St. Frais opened up with one gun on the British position from the tank, killing one soldier and wounding another from the grenadier company of the 39th Regiment on the right of the battalion, whose arm was taken off by a 24lb shot. This was the signal for the opening of the barrage. Upon hearing these shots, the Nawab's artillery in the front line and the curve opened a withering cannonade. A number of Clive's officers wanted to attack the guns, but Clive kept his men together. Most of the shot went over the British, who were now coming to the realisation that the Nawab's artillery was also in place. From the brick-kiln position, the British guns responded, as did the guns with the battalion, but their projectiles failed to injure any of

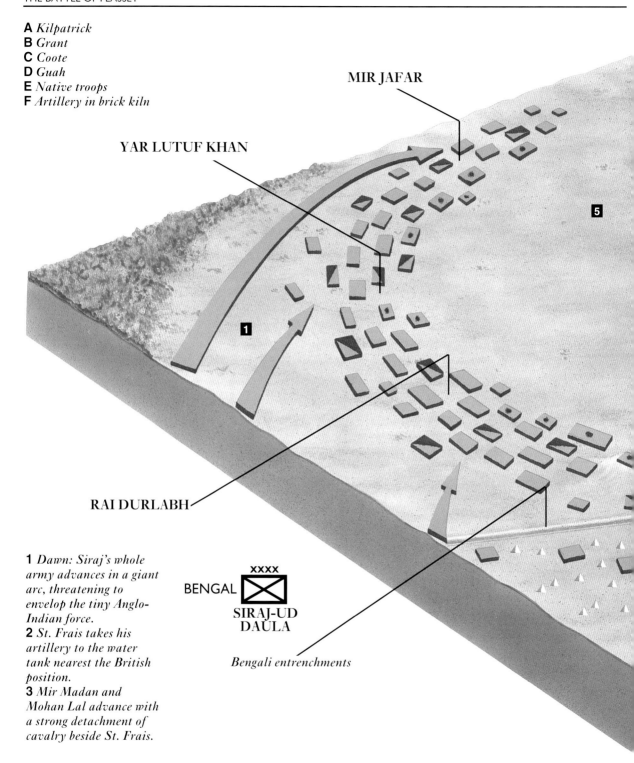

A *Kilpatrick*
B *Grant*
C *Coote*
D *Guah*
E *Native troops*
F *Artillery in brick kiln*

MIR JAFAR

YAR LUTUF KHAN

RAI DURLABH

1 *Dawn: Siraj's whole army advances in a giant arc, threatening to envelop the tiny Anglo-Indian force.*
2 *St. Frais takes his artillery to the water tank nearest the British position.*
3 *Mir Madan and Mohan Lal advance with a strong detachment of cavalry beside St. Frais.*

XXXX
BENGAL ⊠
SIRAJ-UD DAULA

Bengali entrenchments

THE BATTLE OF PLASSEY

Opening deployments and the start of the cannonade, dawn to 8 a.m., 23 June 1757, as seen from the north-west

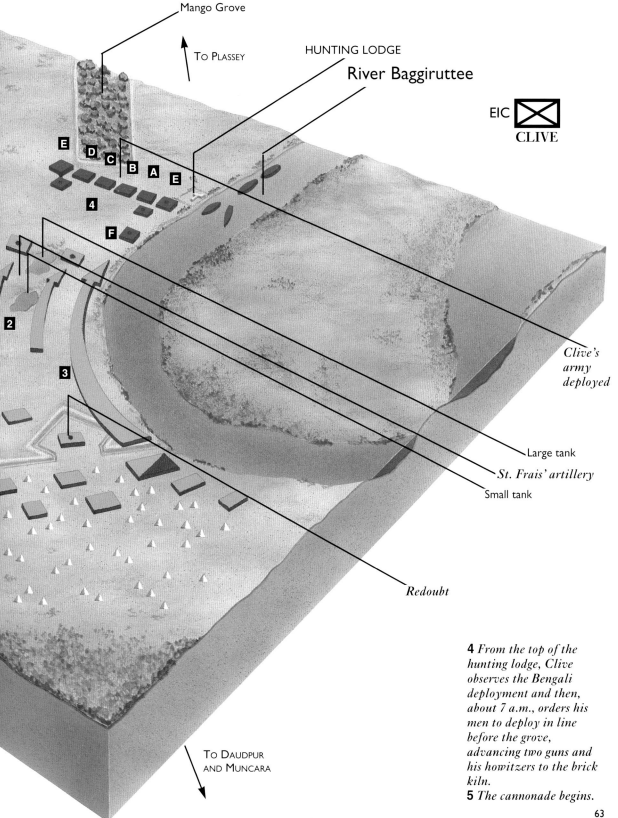

Mango Grove

To Plassey

HUNTING LODGE

River Baggiruttee

EIC

CLIVE

E D C B A E

4

F

2

3

Clive's
army
deployed

Large tank

St. Frais' artillery

Small tank

Redoubt

To Daudpur
and Muncara

4 *From the top of the
hunting lodge, Clive
observes the Bengali
deployment and then,
about 7 a.m., orders his
men to deploy in line
before the grove,
advancing two guns and
his howitzers to the brick
kiln.*
5 *The cannonade begins.*

◀ *Clive on the roof of the Nawab's hunting lodge from a drawing by Richard Caton Woodville published in the* **Illustrated London News** *in 1893. The hunting lodge surrounded by a wall was one of the few buildings on the battlefield, and from its roof Clive surveyed the enemy's position and realised the strength of the Bengali position. Later, after the first attack and a heavy downpour, Clive went into the building to change into drier clothes convinced that a further attack was unlikely. It was here that he was informed apparently about the advance of Kilpatrick's companies. (Anne S. K. Brown Military Collection)*

▼ *The Battle of Plassey by William Harvey as depicted in a woodengraving published in 1853. As there were virtually no contemporary views of the battle, it was left to the imagination of Victorian artists to portray the gallant Clive on a white horse charging into the fray. The picture could not have been further from the truth but such scenes served to create a myth around the battle and Clive. The artist clearly had few details of the battle although he did include the bullocks which hauled the Anglo-Indian guns and was aware that elephants, albeit on the Bengali side, were present at the battle. (Anne S. K. Brown Military Collection, Brown University Library)*

the enemy. Clive's force was receiving casualties, and after half an hour he had lost ten European troops and twenty sepoys. He reacted by shouting an order against the din of the cannon fire to move back into the grove, while the advanced guns remained at the brick-kilns. He was still unclear as to the intentions of the traitors.

Siraj's men, believing their opponents were retreating, moved up their heavy guns and began to pour in a heavy fire, but the shot hit the trees. Clive acknowledged the importance of the sheltered position in his subsequent report: 'Our situation was of the utmost service to us, being lodged in a large grove, with good mud banks.' Occasional explosions of powder were heard coming from Siraj's artillery. Within the grove, the Anglo-Indian force sat down below the banks while others made embrasures in the earth. Once these were completed the artillerymen were able to fire through the holes in the bank, and the guns responded with vigour and considerable effect, killing several of the enemy gunners. Meanwhile the rate of casualties in Clive's force fell off considerably thanks to the protection of the embankment.

◀A Canonnier of the Corps Royal de l'Artillerie of France in 1757. From a watercolour by Keller, c.1890. This figure wears the typical uniform of the period but there are few details of the clothing worn by the small French artillery contingent which fought at Plassey under St. Frais and it is doubtful if their uniforms were as smart and correct as the one depicted in this Victorian image. It is quite probable that most of these men were not trained artillerists at all and one source states that they might have been sailors. (Anne S. K. Brown Military Collection, Brown University Library)

The Death of Mir Madan

This exchange of artillery continued for several hours, neither side making any headway. The Nawab's guns were firing intensely and his position had not faltered under the British fire. Mir Jafar for his part had not made any move and Clive was still unsure of his intentions. He therefore called his staff together at 11 o'clock to discuss the situation. They failed to reach a consensus, so it was decided to persevere with the cannonade until nightfall with an eye to attacking the Nawab's camp at midnight. The position in the grove would be maintained. An hour later, a rumble of thunder announced the onset of a heavy rainstorm which put paid to any prolonged firing from the Bengali guns as most of the

Plassey: The Cannonade

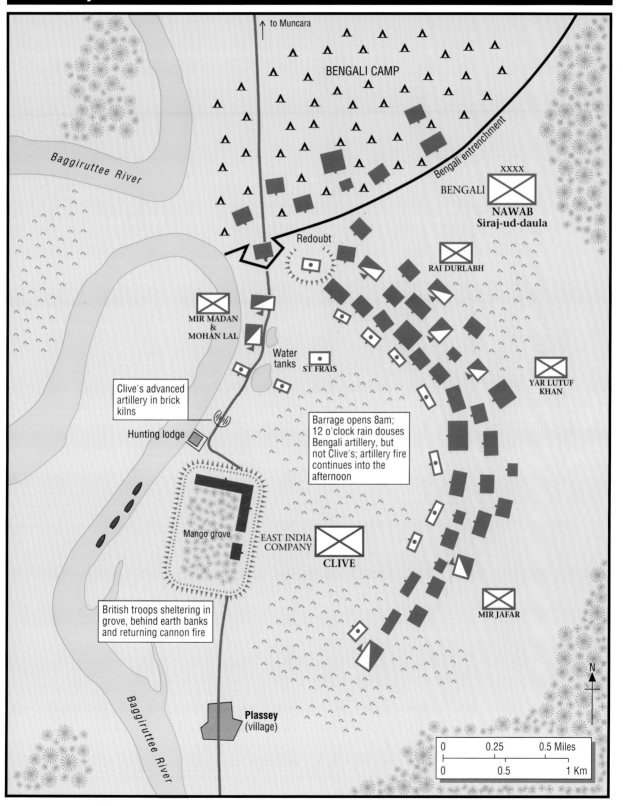

to Muncara

BENGALI CAMP

Baggiruttee River

Bengali entrenchment

BENGALI

XXXX

NAWAB
Siraj-ud-daula

Redoubt

RAI DURLABH

MIR MADAN
&
MOHAN LAL

YAR LUTUF
KHAN

Water
tanks

ST FRAIS

Clive's advanced
artillery in brick
kilns

Hunting lodge

Barrage opens 8am;
12 o'clock rain douses
Bengali artillery, but
not Clive's; artillery fire
continues into the
afternoon

Mango grove

EAST INDIA
COMPANY

CLIVE

MIR JAFAR

British troops sheltering in
grove, behind earth banks
and returning cannon fire

N

Baggiruttee River

Plassey
(village)

| 0 | 0.25 | 0.5 Miles |
| 0 | 0.5 | 1 Km |

◀ *A 19th century engraving of Clive. There are few details as to the appearance of Clive during the battle. It is quite possible that he did not wear the wig so common to the gentry and officers of the 18th century in view of the heat, although military regulation required him to keep up appearances for his men. The only contemporary portraits of Clive from the period of Plassey are the formal paintings in Britain on which this engraving is based. (Anne S. K. Brown Military Collection*

powder got drenched. Some of the Indian artillery tumbrils apparently exploded. While the Indian artillery became sporadic, that of Clive's force continued unabated, their powder and ammunition being covered with tarpaulins during the downpour. For half an hour both sides tried to shelter from the torrential rain.

As the rain began to abate, the Nawab's cavalry under Mir Madan, thinking that the English guns would not be able to continue firing, moved forward from their position near the river to charge, but Mir Madan was killed by a 6-pounder grapeshot and the charge came to nothing. This was a turning-point. While the devoted Mir Madan was alive, Siraj could hope to win the day; now all he had were traitors for generals. Clive himself, convinced that a further attack was unlikely, went down into the hunting lodge to change his sodden clothes, informing his subordinates that he was only to be called if Siraj's army changed its position.

During the cannonade, which continued after the rainstorm until about 3 o'clock, Siraj was in his tent listening intently to the noise of battle and to assurances from his officers – some of whom were

▶*A pencil drawing of a native chieftain thought to be the Nawab of Bengal. During much of the battle, Siraj was away from the action in his tent preferring to leave the command to his lieutenants. Unfortunately, as he was to learn to his cost, several of these were disloyal and were planning his overthrow. Had the Nawab the complete loyalty of his men, the victory at Plassey would have been his and the history of the British in India would have been markedly different. (Anne S. K. Brown Military Collection, Brown University Library)*

traitors – that the victory would be his. Then came word that his most faithful general, Mir Madan, had been mortally wounded. To make matters worse, Behadur Al Khan, the Nawab's son-in-law and one of only three commanders (along with Mir Madan and Mohan Lal) on whom Siraj could depend, was also killed. In fact, it was the troops of these three commanders together with the small French contingent, that fought Clive's force while the rest of the Bengali soldiers, approximately three-quarters of the army, supported the traitors and did not lift a hand to fight.

Moved by these events, the Nawab sent for Mir Jafar and pleaded for forgiveness and begged the latter to defend him. Flinging down his turban at Jafar's feet, Siraj exclaimed, 'Jafar, that turband you must defend', to which the lying Mir Jafar, in a devotional demeanour of hands crossed on breast, promised to lend his full support to the end. It is possible that Mir Jafar had planned to kill the Nawab at this meeting but that there were too many soldiers present. After Jafar's departure, the Nawab now heard from Rai Durlabh (another conspirator) who advised him that no further attempt could be made to attack: the army should be recalled behind the entrenchment and Siraj should return to his capital. Panicked by this, Siraj followed Rai Durlabh's recommendation and ordered his troops under Mohan Lal to retreat to their entrenchment. At first, Lal refused, saying that the fighting was going well, but he eventually agreed. At 2 o'clock, the Indians ceased the cannonade and were seen yoking the trains of oxen to their artillery and moving off towards their camp. Siraj himself sent for his finest dromedary and rode off in great haste with his bodyguard of 2,000 horse to Murshidabad.

The Bengali army was now solely the responsibility of the three treasonous generals. Following his interview with Siraj, Jafar returned to his position and penned a dispatch to Clive informing him of what had transpired and encouraging him to press the attack immediately, and certainly before the next day. But this was not delivered until after the battle as the messenger was reluctant to cross the lines during such a heavy barrage.

Battlefield Manoeuvres

Following the order to retreat into the entrenchment, Mir Jafar's division moved south to be nearer to the Anglo-Indian force, while the bulk of the Nawab's army moved northwards, away from the enemy, leaving St. Frais and his small French contingent alone. Seeing the Bengali forces retiring, leaving the French detachment isolated, the hotheaded Major Kilpatrick, who had taken temporary charge of the British force while Clive was inside the hunting lodge, advanced towards the larger of the two water tanks with two companies of the 39th Regiment, totalling 250 men, and two guns to attack St. Frais. If this position could be taken, it would allow Clive's artillery to cannonade the retreating enemy. Kilpatrick also sent a soldier to alert Clive.

Legend has it that the man found Clive asleep in the hunting lodge. In the words of Orme, 'Some say he was asleep; which is not improbable, considering how little rest he had had for so many hours

before; but this is no imputation either against his courage or conduct.' Upon hearing the news however, Clive sprang up in anger at the action of one of his officers without his orders. As soon as he saw the position, Clive realised that he would have acted in the same way had he been on the spot. Moving up to the companies, he nevertheless reprimanded Kilpatrick and ordered him back in order to bring up the rest of the force, so that he could have the glory of leading the advance. The water tank was taken about 3 o'clock after St. Frais and his men fell back with their guns to the entrenchment, but not before they fired a parting shot. Once

▼ *The Battle of Plassey as depicted in a fanciful watercolour by E. S. Hardy painted around 1900. Most of the hand-to-hand fighting was short-lived and occurred during the taking of the tanks and the eventual occupation of the redoubt. According to the contemporary accounts, the British troops encountered little resistance from the Indians. (Anne S. K. Brown Military Collection, Brown University Library)*

▶ *A manuscript entitled* **Plan and Prospect of the Battle of Plassey the 23 June 1757 between the English and the Nabob of Bengal gained by Colonel Clive Commander in Chief of the English Forces there.** *The artist of this picture and maps is unknown but this is the only contemporary view of the battle and the three maps have been the main source for the movements of the armies during the battle. The artist clearly had some details of the event and may have been a participant. The elephants are clearly depicted as is the grove and hunting lodge. The manuscript is now in the India Office Library. (The British Library)*

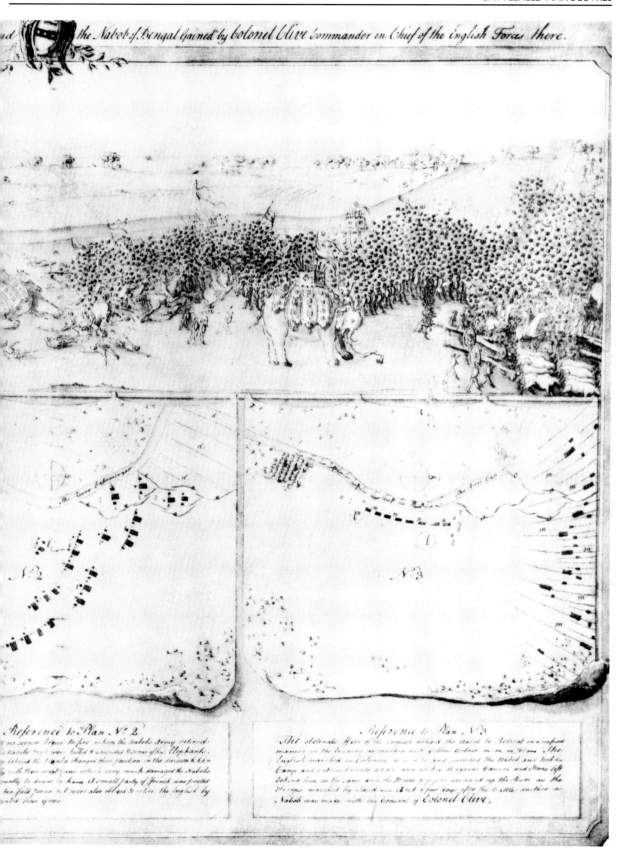

◀ A suit of elephant armour now in the Tower of London and thought to have been a trophy won by Clive at Plassey although the exact provenance is unclear and its connection with the battle is questionable. Interestingly, in the manuscript illustration, the elephants do not appear to be wearing any armour. (Anne S. K. Brown Military Collection, Brown University Library)

▲ A Victorian illustration of an elephant for battle, with armour howdah, etc. (Cassell's Illustrated History of India)

back in the defences, St. Frais established his battery in a redoubt situated at the corner of the earthwork.

Two of Siraj's divisions were now returning to the entrenchment. The third under Mir Jafar still lingered in its original position before gradually moving northwards, reaching a point in line with the northern end of the grove and then advancing towards the north-east angle. Clive had no idea who was in charge of this wing and saw the urgency to prevent any further advance. Fearing for the safety of his baggage, he dispatched three platoons under the command of Captain Grant and Lieutenant Rumbold and a field piece manned by a volunteer, John Johnstone, to check them. Several shots from this gun halted any further offensive movements by the Indians.

Clive now hoped to draw the enemy back out of their entrenchment and indeed, the French 'put some courage into their troops again' by encouraging the remnants of the Nawab's force who were still loyal to advance towards the Anglo-Indian force while St. Frais's guns fired from their new position. In addition, there was a cavalry charge, but this was kept at bay by musket and cannon fire from Clive's guns, which were quickly advanced to the position. However, some of the Bengalis moved towards a strong position around a small hillock to harass Clive's men. He moved half his infantry and half his artillery to the smaller of the two water tanks which had been taken earlier by grenadiers from the 39th, and the other half to rising ground 200 yards to the left of it. From the two water tanks and the rising ground Clive's guns started to bombard the entrenchment.

Four more Bengali officers were killed and confusion rained on the Nawab's camp as the elephants, according to one witness, 'grew very unruly' and began to stampede. Some of the ammunition blew up. St. Frais continued to fire his guns and the Nawab's soldiers shot off their matchlocks from

▼A highly imaginative 19th century representation of the battle of Plassey showing Clive on a horse leading his men into close combat with the Bengalis. There is no evidence to suggest that Clive was mounted at any time during the battle. Indeed, the Anglo-Indian army may have lacked horses altogether, although Clive most likely travelled on horseback before and after the battle. As with much of the background to the battle, such details are vague. (Anne S. K. Brown Military Collection, Brown University Library)

every conceivable position in ditches, hollows and holes and from bushes on the hillock east of the redoubt 150 yards from the forward British position, while some cavalry advanced several times threatening to charge. All was in vain under the withering fire from the Anglo-Indian troops. It was during this phase of the battle, however, that Clive's force sustained most of its casualties. There was wholescale confusion as the leaderless Indians struggled to maintain their positions. Some coolies who tried to bring guns into action with oxen were shot down.

Mir Jafar's troops had been not been engaged at any point in the proceedings and had not moved from their position since being fired on by the field piece. It was only as they now began to leave the field that Clive realised they must be Mir Jafar's soldiers. Greatly relieved and safe in the knowledge that his flank and rear were safe, Clive could now

▲ *Medal struck in commemoration of the Victory at Plassey issued in 1758. Another medal was issued by the East India Company in 1766 bearing a portrait of Clive on one side with the words 'ROBERT CLIVE BARON OF PLASSEY', while on the reverse stands an angelic figure by a tall pyramid bearing details of the victory and the establishment of peace in Bengal surrounded by the words 'HONOUR THE REWARD OF MERIT'. (Anne S. K. Brown Military Collection, Brown University Library)*

As Coote's force advanced they noticed a large body of horse on their right, 'and upon our firing some shot at them, a messenger arrived with a letter to the Colonel from Meer Jaffier, acquainting him that he – Meer Jaffier – commanded that body, and requesting an interview with him that night or the next morning'.

The Close of the Battle

The last to leave the entrenchment were the French soldiers. Having been outnumbered ten to one, but having lost a mere handful of men, the Anglo-Indian force moved forward and occupied the earthwork and camp, with its considerable booty at 5 o'clock. According to Orme, 'the English soldiers being told, that they should receive a donation of money, received the orders to march on to Daudpore with acclamations, nor shewed any desire to stop for the plunder which lay spread around them'. They did halt to allow the commissaries to take possession of enough oxen to haul the various guns and carriages, the animals in the Nawab's camp being superior to those the British had been using. Siraj's army was meanwhile in complete disarray and making off in all directions. The small Anglo-Indian force had performed admirably. Their arms and equipment had not been superior to that of the

focus all his efforts on dislodging the French from the redoubt and the party of matchlockmen and a large body of cavalry situated on the hillock to the east of it. Two grenadier companies of the 39th, 160 men in all, under Coote were sent against the hillock on the right while simultaneously another detachment assaulted the redoubt, supported by the main force, which advanced in the centre. As Coote's troops moved towards the position, the enemy bolted without firing a shot and the hillock was taken around 4.30 p.m. In the words of Coote: 'Perceiving the enemy retire on all sides, I was ordered to march into their lines, which I entered without opposition.' Coote pursued the Bengalis over the entrenchment. St. Frais, realising his predicament, alone and abandoned, had no alternative but to retreat, also abandoning his guns.

1 *After the death of Mir Madan and his meeting with Mir Jafar, Siraj orders the Bengali army to withdraw.*
2 *The Nawab makes off with his bodyguard of 2,000 cavalry, leaving his army to shift for itself.*

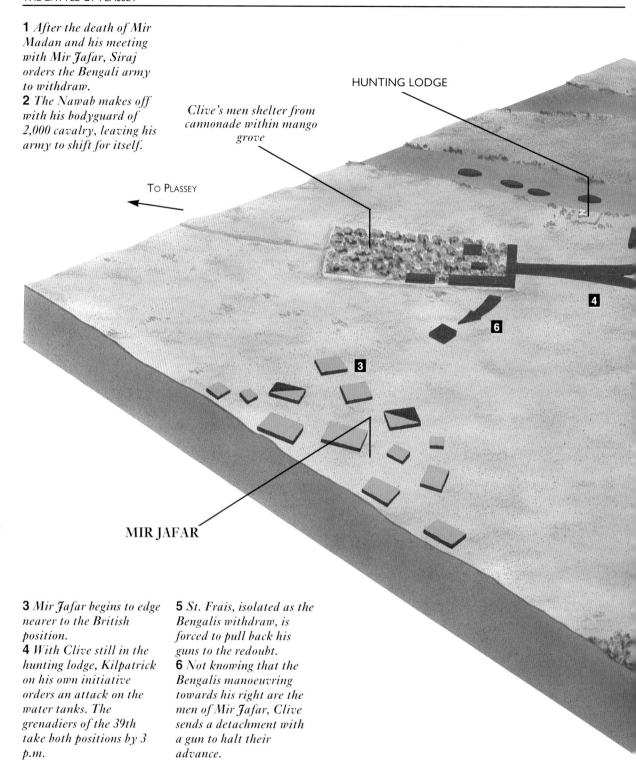

HUNTING LODGE

Clive's men shelter from cannonade within mango grove

TO PLASSEY

MIR JAFAR

3 *Mir Jafar begins to edge nearer to the British position.*
4 *With Clive still in the hunting lodge, Kilpatrick on his own initiative orders an attack on the water tanks. The grenadiers of the 39th take both positions by 3 p.m.*

5 *St. Frais, isolated as the Bengalis withdraw, is forced to pull back his guns to the redoubt.*
6 *Not knowing that the Bengalis manoeuvring towards his right are the men of Mir Jafar, Clive sends a detachment with a gun to halt their advance.*

THE BATTLE OF PLASSEY

The Bengali withdrawal and Clive's attack, as seen from the north-east

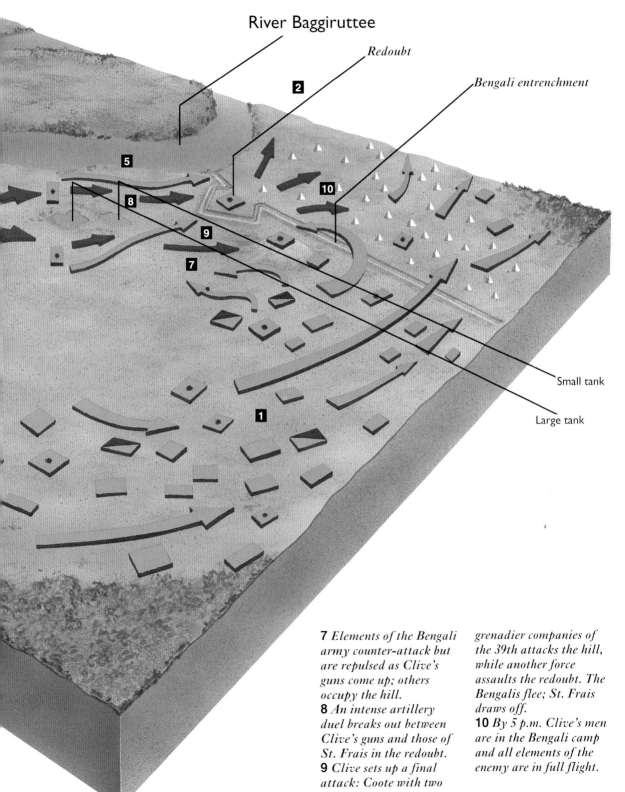

River Baggiruttee

Redoubt

2

Bengali entrenchment

5

8

10

9

7

Small tank

1

Large tank

7 *Elements of the Bengali army counter-attack but are repulsed as Clive's guns come up; others occupy the hill.*
8 *An intense artillery duel breaks out between Clive's guns and those of St. Frais in the redoubt.*
9 *Clive sets up a final attack: Coote with two*

grenadier companies of the 39th attacks the hill, while another force assaults the redoubt. The Bengalis flee; St. Frais draws off.
10 *By 5 p.m. Clive's men are in the Bengali camp and all elements of the enemy are in full flight.*

enemy, but they had demonstrated the importance of discipline, confidence and high morale under fire. Perhaps more importantly, the battle had shown the importance of native troops, a point previously ignored by the British authorities but which was quickly exploited to the fullest.

Siraj had fled to Murshidabad accompanied by about 2,000 horsemen, having lost an estimated 500 men among whom were some of his most important officers. As the British and sepoys occupied the camp, Mir Jafar's letter finally arrived. It went as follows:

'Your note is arrived. I was in the Nabob's presence on this plain, and observed that everybody was intimidated. He sent for me and flung his turband off before me, and one day he made me write on the side of the Koran, so that I cannot come over to you. By the blessing of God you have the better of the day. Meer Madan was wounded by a ball and is since dead. Buxshee Hazarry is killed, and ten or fifteen horsemen are killed and wounded. Roydullubram, Luttee Codair Cawn, and myself are moved from right to left. Make a great and sudden discharge and they shall run away and we shall do our part. The commanders of the foot and the swordsmen have left the entrenchments, leaving the guns there. I have mentioned but a small part of the loss of that part of the army commanded by Meer Madan has sustained. Had you taken that opportunity to advance with your army there had been nothing more to do. It grieves me that I was then at a distance.'

Mir Jafar finished his letter by urging Clive to attack at 3 o'clock the next morning. This was now unnecessary, and Clive responded by sending word that he would meet Mir Jafar next day at Daudpore. He then ordered Coote in the absence of cavalry to take a small force and pursue the remnants of the enemy as fast as their tired legs could carry them. They were also sent to observe any signs of the enemy rallying. Eventually tiredness won the day and Coote had to halt his men at Daudpore six miles from the battlefield.

It had been a relatively bloodless battle, the outcome decided more by the treacherous acts of Mir Jafar, Rai Durlabh and others than by any decisive force of arms. Had there been no conspiracy, Clive's little force would not have stood a chance and would have been easily enveloped had Siraj chosen to advance. But morale in the Nawab's army had been low, and the death of Mir Madan had dealt Siraj a shocking blow.

In terms of its political consequences, it had been a most decisive victory. In the words of Fortescue, 'It was a small price to pay for dominion over the provinces of Bengal, Orissa, and Behar, for such and no less were the fruits of victory. Yet it is not by the mere tale of the slaughtered and maimed that such successes must be judged. The victory may have been easily won when the moment came for the actual clash of arms; but the main point is that the British were there to win it. The campaign of Plassey is less a study of military skill than of the iron will and unshaken nerve that could lead three thousand men against a host of unknown strength, and hold them, undaunted, a single slender line, within a ring of fifty thousand enemies.' It was by no means a straightforward military victory. Deception had played a decisive part, as Malleson concluded: 'No unbiased Englishmen, sitting in judgement on the events which passed in the interval between 9th February and the 23rd June, can deny that the name of Siraju'd daulah stands higher in the scale of honour than does the name of Clive. He was the only one of the principal actors in that tragic drama who did not attempt to deceive!'

THE AFTERMATH OF THE BATTLE

Considering the scale of the battle's impact on the future of India, Plassey resulted in very few casualties. According to Clive's dispatches of 2 July 1757 to the Madras Council and his letter to the East India Company on 26 July, the total losses suffered by the Anglo-Indian force were estimated at 22 killed and 50 wounded; the killed being 'chiefly Blacks'. Orme states that 20 Europeans were killed or wounded, 16 sepoys killed and 36 wounded. Of the Europeans, 6 of the fatalities and 12 of the wounded, including the only two officers wounded in the action, came from the artillery contingent (although authorities differ on whether they were all from the artillery). However, in the return of Clive's force taken at Murshidabad dated 3 August 1757, the casualties of 23 June are listed along with their units. According to this, of the killed, three were of the Madras Artillery, one of the Madras regiment, and one of the Bengal Europeans; 15

other ranks are listed as wounded, of which four were of the 39th Regiment, three of the Madras Regiment, two of the Bengal Europeans, four of the Madras Artillery, one of the Bengal Artillery

▼*A view of Calcutta taken from Fort William from an engraving by W. Byrne from a picture by W. Hodges, published in 1793. Calcutta was the key to Bengal and was fought over several times throughout the 1750s. With the victory at Plassey, it became the most important city in India, and Bengal the most important province. Even Bombay never achieved the fame bestowed on Calcutta, which became endowed with some fine public buildings including Fort William, which was rebuilt several times. Contrasting with these fine buildings were the massive shanty-town areas housing India's poor which grew up within the city. (Anne S. K. Brown Military Collection, Brown University Library)*

and one of the Bombay Regiment. The list names three officers who were wounded: Lieutenants De Lubers of the Bengal European Regiment, Cassells of the Bengal Artillery and Holst, probably of the Bengal Artillery, the latter apparently dying later and being buried in Calcutta on 13 November. Four Madras sepoys are listed as killed and 19 wounded, while the Bengal sepoys lost 9 killed and 11 wounded. One sailor, a Mr. Shoreditch from HMS *Kent* was wounded while serving with the artillery and other naval personnel may have been wounded.

Clive estimated that the Nawab lost 500 men, not a large proportion of his considerable army; the loss of several important officers including Mir Madan and Buxshee Hazarry proved critical, however, to the outcome of the battle.

▶ *A view of Fort St. George, Madras as it appeared after the siege of 1759. The victory at Plassey did not mean the arrival of peace in India and fighting continued on and off between the British, French and their respective Indian confederates for many more years. Fort St. George was besieged by the French from November 1758 until February 1759. (Anne S. K. Brown Military Collection, Brown University Library)*

The victorious force halted on the battlefield long enough to secure fresh bullocks to pull the guns, before pressing on with the pursuit. They finally halted at midnight near the village of Daudpore. Mir Jafar spent most of the night at Plassey. During that evening after the battle, Clive sent the following note to Watson and the Committee at Fort William:

'Gentlemen – This morning at one o'clock we arrived at Placis Grove and early in the morning the Nabob's whole army appeared in sight and cannonaded us for several hours, and about noon returned to a very strong camp in sight, lately Roydoolub's, upon which we advanced and stormed the Nabob's camp, which we have taken with all his cannon and

◀ *The meeting of Clive and Mir Jafar after the battle of Plassey, in a scene painted around 1760 by Francis Hayman. Surprisingly, the victory at Plassey failed to excite the imagination of contemporary painters unlike the death of Wolfe at Quebec in 1759 or the capture of Havana in 1762.*

This painting by Hayman was originally commissioned for a new Rotunda Saloon at Vauxhall Gardens. The artist also painted a scene of the surrender of Pondicherry to Colonel Eyre Coote in January 1761. (National Portrait Gallery, London)

pursued him six miles, being now at Doudpoor and shall proceed for Muxadavad tomorrow. Meer Jaffeir, Roydoolub, and Luttee Cawn gave us no other assistance than standing neutral. They are with me with a large force. Meer Muddun and five hundred horse are killed and three elephants. Our loss is trifling, not above twenty Europeans killed and wounded.'

Sometime the same evening Clive received a congratulatory message from Mir Jafar, who asked that Clive send Watts or two other persons to meet him at his camp. The general sent Omar Beg and Luke Scrafton on the following morning to bring Mir Jafar to Daudpur. With an honour guard drawn out for his reception, Mir Jafar entered the town and met Clive, who embraced him and addressed him as the new Nawab, advising him to head for the capital as quickly as possible. Following closely behind, Clive reached Mandipur before moving on to Murshidabad. He had been warned about a possible attempt upon his life, and when he arrived in the city on the 29 June he was well guarded by an escort of 200 European soldiers and 300 sepoys. In the afternoon, Clive met Mir Jafar again in the throne room of the Royal palace, where tradition was acted out by Clive submitting to the

◀ *Hyder Ali, chief of the Mahrattas against the British in 1761. Engraving after J. Year. Having consolidated Bengal with the victory at Plassey, the British sought to take Madras. This led to a series of bitterly contested wars with the powerful state of Mysore under its leader Hyder Ali and his son Tipu Sultan, culminating in the final British victory at Seringapatam in 1799 where Tipu Sultan was killed. (Anne S. K. Brown Military Collection, Brown University Library)*

Mir Jafar as Subah by presenting a few pieces of gold.

Following the battle of Plassey, Siraj fled to Murshidabad where he had the doors of his treasury opened in the hope of inducing his soldiers to continue their support, but no avail. Several of his officers suggested that he surrender himself to Clive, but the former Nawab dismissed such treasonable talk. Hearing of the arrival of Mir Jafar in the city around midnight, he fled, placing Lutfennessa his consort, 'and a number of favourites into coaches and covered chairs, loaded them with as much gold and as many jewels as they could contain, and taking with him a number of elephants, with his best baggage and furniture'. He was hotly

pursued by a party of soldiers but managed to reach the area around Raj Mahal, where he was betrayed after seeking refuge in the house of a man whom he had previously arrested and punished for some offence – the man sent word to the local military governor, who was the brother of Mir Jafar, and Siraj was taken into custody. A council headed by Mir Jafar met to decide what to do with him but failed to reach a decision. He was placed in the custody of Mir Jafar's son, Miran, who had Siraj murdered that night. His mutilated body was carried through the streets of Murshidabad on the back of an elephant on 3 July 1757. He had received his just deserts, as one one Indian historian observed: 'Siraj-ud-daula had attained the zenith of power and opulence, and therefore a declension was inevitable according to the laws of nature.' He died without knowing that a French force under Law had been dispatched to try and save him and were in fact only two days' march from rescuing him.

The British were now the paramount colonial force in the subcontinent. With the French eclipsed by Clive's success, only the Dutch remained in the subcontinent to be reckoned with. Encouraged by Mir Jafar, soon chafing at his subordinate role to the British, the Dutch sent troops from Batavia to their settlement on the Hooghly at Chinsura. Under the command of Colonel Francis Forde, a small Anglo-Indian force defeated a slightly larger Dutch-Malay army at Badara on 25 November 1759. While Bengal was now firmly in the hands of the British, Madras was still coveted by the French, and several naval skirmishes took place off the Coromandel coast. Fort St. David was attacked and taken in early June 1758 by Comte Thomas-Arthur Lally de Tollendal, who had designs to drive the British out of Madras. In November 1758, the French moved on Madras and began siege operations against the town

until the appearance of a British squadron under Sir George Pocock on 16 February forced them to withdraw. This was not the end of French ambitions, and the campaign known as the Third Carnatic War continued, this time in the areas of the Deccan and Hyderabad, where the British were again successful. In 1761 Pondicherry was the scene of yet another battle, when Eyre Coote defeated a French garrison under Lally, who was supported by Hyder Ali, commander of the Mysore forces, thus effectively closing the French colonial era in India.

▼ **The Peace Makers of India,** *a contemporary engraving published in 1768 showing representatives of the East India Company in Madras kneeling before Hyder Ali. Behind the Indian leader stand General Smith, the English commander, his hands tied behind him, looking resentfully at the proceedings. The caricature rep-* *resents the peace concluded by the English with Hyder Ali of Mysore at Madras in 1768. The peace was short-lived, for a later ruler of Mysore, Tipu Sultan, was to be a thorn in the side of England for many years in the 1790s. (Anne S. K. Brown Military Collection, Brown University Library)*

◀ *The siege of Pondicherry in 1778 as depicted in 1902 by Henri Dupray. The competition between France and Britain in the Carnatic involved numerous attacks and sieges upon each other's centres. Pondicherry, the main French base in the area, withstood a siege of 50 days by Admiral Boscawen in 1748. It was again besieged by Coote in 1761, and by Sir Hector Munro in 1778. It was restored to France in 1783 but was captured by Britain ten years later, and it was not until 1816 that it reverted back to French governorship. (Anne S. K. Brown Military Collection, Brown University Library)*

At the Treaty of Paris in 1763, the French were given custody of Pondicherry, but they never again became a major threat to British interests. In the end, that skirmish in the grove of palas trees in 1757 proved to be the turning-point for British fortunes in India. From being simple merchants they would emerge as rulers of a great empire and to dominate India for almost two centuries.

A symbolic picture by Henry Darien representing the end of French India, showing a lone French sentry standing amidst the ruins of a building with several of his colleagues lying dead or dying, while in the background a city burns. (Anne S. K. Brown Military Collection, Brown University Library)

▲The French commissioners at the surrender of Pondicherry in 1761.

▼'Clive receives the grant of Bengal and Orissa at Allahabad August 1765': the third bas relief panel on the base of the Clive statue in Westminster. (DAG)

THE BATTLEFIELD TODAY

Following Indian independence in 1948, many of the battlefields connected with British supremacy were neglected including those monuments that had been erected by the former colonial government. While the field of Plassey suffered to a small extent from this, the major transformations to the ground were natural. In 1899, a visitor to Plassey remarked: 'The fame of the Battle of Plassey has outlasted the field upon which it was fought, for the river Bhagirathi [*sic*] has been steadily eating away the plain. In 1801 there were 3,000 trees remaining in Clive's famous grove; eighty years later only *one* remained, beneath which were buried the remains of one of the Nawab's generals who fell in the battle. The greater part of Plassey is covered by the waters of the river, and the remainder has lapsed into jungle.'

According to Edwardes, 'the site of the battlefield is so much changed today [1963] that none of the features described by eye-witnesses can be properly identified'. The river has changed its course considerably over the last two hundred years and altered the surrounding terrain. Today, the visitor

▼ *The Nawab's shooting lodge, Plassey, as depicted in an early 19th century watercolour by Captain James Blunt who served with the Bengal Engineers from 1783 to 1810. This is one of the few actual views of the area around Plassey,* *which has since changed considerably owing to the varying course of the river over the last two hundred years. Today nothing remains of Plassey House, and evidence of the grove has been completely obliterated. (The British Library)*

arriving at the site is first met by a large obelisk emblazoned with the name 'PLASSEY', which was erected during the days of the Raj but is now suffering from decay. A small group of rural huts and some former British bungalows stand on the edge of the battlefield near a small pond. Nearby stuck into the earth are several small metal pegs bearing legends such as 'Forward Position of British Guns'. There is also a large memorial to the Moghul army, but this too is in a state of decay.

While there are no contemporary pictures of the battlefield other than the illustration in the manuscript in the India Office Library, two early nineteenth century British artists visited Plassey. James Tillyer Blunt (1765–1834) served with the Bengal Engineers and spent considerable time surveying parts of India in the 1790s and in the first years of the nineteenth century. One of his watercolour and ink drawings depicted the ruins of Plassey House (the Nawab's shooting lodge) and the grove in 1800. Thomas Daniell painted a view of Plassey from upriver showing some later buildings.

Some artifacts including standards from the battle are housed in the old palace at Murshidabad, but the majority of relics are now in various British collections.

In Britain, there are some reminders of the battle fought thousands of miles away. At Lydbury North in Shropshire, in the parkland adjacent to the house that was once owned by Clive, a group of trees half a mile long were planted on a hillside so as to form the letters of the word 'Plassey'. In the same county is Styche Hall, north of the village of Moreton Say, where Clive was born; the school at Market Drayton which he attended; and there is a statue to him in Shrewsbury. Items relating to Clive in India can be seen at Powis Castle, while the Royal Armouries in the Tower of London has several items of Indian armour from the period, including the famous elephant chain mail. Eyre Coote is buried in Rockburne, Hampshire, and a pillar erected by the East India Company stands in the grounds of his house.

CHRONOLOGY

Events leading to the Battle of Plassey
2 January 1757 Calcutta reoccupied.
5 February Attack on Siraj's camp in Calcutta.
9 February Treaty between Siraj-ud-daula and East India Company restoring position of Calcutta.
23 March Chandernagore taken.
19 May True and false treaties drawn up with Mir Jafar and signed by Calcutta Council.
5 June Mir Jafar signs treaty.
13 June Clive begins his march northwards.
17 June Coote captures Cutna Fort.
19 June Clive arrives at Katwa.
21 June Clive holds his first and only Council of War.
22 June Clive's force crosses Hooghly river.
4 p.m. March towards Plassey begins.
6 p.m. Clive sends reply to Mir Jafar.
23 June BATTLE OF PLASSEY:
Midnight Advanced troops arrive.
3 a.m. Clive's rearguard arrives at Plassey.
Dawn Clive surveys scene from rooftop of hunting lodge.
7 a.m. Clive sends note to Mir Jafar.
c.7 a.m. Cannonade commences.
c.11 a.m. Mir Madan leads attack on grove and is mortally wounded.
12 a.m. Heavy rainstorm drenches the battlefield.
2 p.m. Cannonade ceases. Clive moves to the brick house to change his clothes.

*c.***2 p.m.** Kilpatrick advances with two guns towards water tank.
*c.***3 p.m.** Clive assumes command and takes water tank.
*c.***3 p.m.** Nawab's cavalry and infantry make move but kept at bay.
*c.***3 p.m.** Clive's troops harassed from force at second water tank. This force attacked and driven out of position.
*c.***4 p.m.** Advance of Mir Jafar's troops towards Clive's position.
*c.***4 30 p.m.** Anglo-Indian force charges Nawab's position. Flight of Nawab's army.
5 p.m. General rout of Nawab's army.
5 p.m. Mir Jafar's letter arrives.
Midnight Siraj arrives at Murshidabad.
29 June Mir Jafar installed as Nawab.

November 1757 to May 1758
Operations in Bihar.

Events following the Battle of Plassey
23 June, midnight Siraj arrives at Murshidabad.
24 June Clive meets Mir Jafar.
24 June Mir Jafar enters Murshidabad; Siraj flees.
29 June Anglo-Indian army enters Murshidabad.
2 July Siraj brought to Murshidabad and killed.
3 July Mutilated body of Nawab paraded through the city.

A GUIDE
TO FURTHER READING

The best contemporary account of Plassey and the various campaigns in India in the 1750s is Edward Orme's *A History of the Military Transactions of the British Nation in Indostan from the Year MDCCXLV*, London, 1778. The battle is discussed in many sources including G. B. Malleson's *The Decisive Battles of India*, London, 1885, and more recently in *The Battle of Plassey and the Conquest of Bengal* by Michael Edwardes, London, 1963.

For the various forces that fought at Plassey, the best sources for the British regiments are C. T. Atkinson, *The Dorset Regiment*, Volume 1, Oxford, 1947; *Historical Record of The Honourable East India Company's First Madras European Regiment*, London, 1843; *Neill's 'Blue Caps'* (Vol. 1 1639–1826) by H. C. Wylly, Aldershot, *c*.1923; and F. G. Cardew's *A Sketch of the Services of the Bengal Native Army to*

the Year 1895, Calcutta, 1903. Nothing detailed exists for the Nawab's army.

For biographical details of Clive, there is a range of books, some of the best being *Clive of India* by Nirad C. Chaudhuri, London, 1975; Mark Bence-Jones's book of the same title, *Clive of India*, New York, 1974; and *Clive of Plassey* by A. Mervyn Davies, New York, 1939. For Coote, see *A Life of Lieutenant-General Sir Eyre Coote, K.B.* compiled by H. C. Wylly, Oxford, 1922. Nothing exists in terms of biographical notes for Siraj-ud-daula.

For the political events surrounding Plassey, the best source is a volume in the Indian Records Series entitled *Bengal in 1756–1757*, edited by S. C. Hill, London, 1905. This contains a selection of public and private papers dealing with the affairs of the British in Bengal during the reign of Siraj-ud-daula.

WARGAMING PLASSEY

Small Wars, the classic British study of colonial warfare, was written in the 1890s by Major Charles Callwell and reprinted many times before 1914. He argued that in colonial battles, from the plains of India to the jungles of Africa, small European forces had achieved victory by assuming the offensive, whatever the odds. 'The records of small wars', he observed, 'show unmistakably how great is the impression made upon semi-civilised races and upon savages by a bold and resolute procedure. The military history of our Indian Empire affords proof of this in every page. From the days of Clive down to the present time victory has been achieved by vigour and by dash rather than by force of numbers. The spirit of the attack inspiring leaders and subordinates alike has won the day for us.' He went on to cite Arcot, Plassey and Meani as classic examples. At Meani (also rendered as Meeanee) in 1843, Sir Charles Napier defeated an estimated 30,000 Baluchis with just 2,600 European troops and sepoys. He described the splendid appearance of the enemy: 'Thick as standing corn and gorgeous as a field of flowers stood the Baluchis, in their many coloured garments and turbans. Guarding their heads with their long dark shields, they shook their sharp swords gleaming in the sun, their shouts rolling like a peal of thunder, as with frantic gestures they dashed forward with demoniac strength and ferocity, full against the front of the 22nd.' Which is where they went wrong. The undaunted Irish regulars gave them a volley then waded in with the bayonet. After several hours, thousands of Baluchis lay dead and another colonial campaign had ended in victory.

Indian Armies

Ferocity is not a feature of the Nawab's army at Plassey. Indeed, the marked reluctance of Siraj's soldiers to enter the fray all but decided the battle.

Yet it does make an incredibly colourful spectacle on a wargame table. I decided to organise an Indian army many years ago after seeing the diorama in the Devon & Dorset's museum at Dorchester castle. Masses of turbaned warriors, hordes of cavalry with armoured elephants and monstrous ox-drawn cannon; they may have been impractical, and ultimately unsuccessful, but the armies of the eighteenth century Nawabs do look magnificent.

Given the poor showing of most of the Nawab's troops at Plassey, you may not feel willing to devote much time and money to recreating his motley army on the tabletop. My solution was to assemble a more 'general purpose' force that serves for a variety of historical periods. The core of my 15mm army is a group of desperate cut-throats culled from various manufacturers: the figures include Afghan tribesmen, Sudanese riflemen, Arabs from the Crusades and First World War as well as various conversions. They look equally at home on the rocky crags of the North West Frontier, outside the walls of Khartoum, or as irregular forces in the Balkans and the Caucasus, fighting for or against my 15-mm Turkish troops. By adding mailed horsemen (who double as Emirs in my Sudanese army) and elephants from my ancient Persians, I can march them on the field of Plassey. This may not be music to the ears of figure manufacturers, but it has enabled me to wargame all sorts of esoteric periods without buying and painting too many specific figures.

Although the exact order of battle of the Nawab's army is unknown today (and it was probably a mystery to him too), it was typical of the eighteenth century Indian armies. The great mass of infantry were little more than watchmen to look after the baggage. Cavalry remained the principal arm, with colourful and noisy – if ineffective – support from the elephants. As we have seen, the artillery was practically immobile and only really dangerous when served by French gunners. However, the soldiers were but pawns in the endless political struggles between princes, generals and courtiers. Each band of horsemen might owe loyalty to the leader who recruited them, but they had no sense of wider loyalty to the Nawab or to the Moghul Emperor.

The effective desertion of Mir Jafar was undoubtedly the turning-point at Plassey, but it was not an unusual act in itself. Indeed, in most major battles in India during the seventeenth and eighteenth centuries, one or more nobles changed sides or refused to commit his forces. Such treachery was an almost standard feature of Indian military life, the natural consequence of the courtiers' preoccupation with *hasad-wa-fasad* (jealousy and intrigue). What might have happened if, contrary to its nature, Siraj-ud-daula's army had launched a united attack on Clive's outnumbered force? Napier's experience at Meani suggests that Clive would probably have won, although British casualties would have been higher. Siraj's soldiers had only the most rudimentary organisation and could not deliver the sort of concentrated, coordinated assault that might have overwhelmed the thin line of sepoys and British infantry.

The Moghul armies were fragile organisations, terribly vulnerable to the loss of a few key leaders. Later British observers were always pleased to see the enemy leaders riding to war in traditional splendour, directing operations from an elephant's *howdah* – a single well-aimed 6-pounder cannon ball could literally behead the Indian army before the fighting had really started.

Siraj-ud-daula knew there was every chance of his army disintegrating in battle as a result of internal rivalries; but he was also aware that, even if Mir Jafar kept some of his promises, the army could still be defeated by a much smaller number of Europeans and sepoys. At San Thome, eleven years earlier, 700 French-trained sepoys and 230 French infantry had attacked and defeated a far larger Indian force – perhaps 10,000 strong. The French had no artillery; the Indians had occupied a defensive position and dotted it with large cannon. Siraj's more learned courtiers may have wondered whether history was repeating itself: after all, the Moghul Empire had been created after the Battle of Panipat in 1526, when a modest force of Moghul cavalry defeated an Indian army that outnumbered it 10:1. Now a new set of foreign conquerors had appeared, also with small but apparently superior armies.

The Art of the Possible

Since the military capability of Siraj's army is so limited, refighting Plassey as a straightforward tactical exercise is unlikely to be particularly challenging. It could obviously be run as a 'multi-player solo game', with players representing Clive, his subordinates and other officials of the East India Company. While the Indian army is controlled by the umpire, the players jockey for position, each with his own personal victory conditions. Remember that Clive's troubles were by no means over after his triumph at Plassey. Admiral Watson had his supporters, and Clive received a mixed reception back in England, where tales of oriental corruption sullied his name and would eventually drive him to a third (and successful) suicide attempt. Although Clive was later venerated as a hero in Victorian times, writers were often uncomfortable when it came to admitting that Clive had outplayed the treacherous Indian princes at their own game. A typical popular history, *Our Empire Story*, said of the fake treaty given to Omichand, 'Of course this was wrong, and this deed shows like a black dot among all the splendid and brave acts of Clive's life. But the position of the British in India was full of danger. They were but a handful of white men in the midst of millions of dark foes, and Clive thought that it would only be by meeting treachery by treachery that he could save them all from death.'

While the internal politics of the East India Company could make a fine role-playing game, Siraj's court offers even greater possibilities. That perfumed world of oriental corruption and decadence, bribery, flattery and treachery is peopled with larger-than-life characters, all far more interesting than the characterless Eurocrats that preside over western politics today. I would be inclined to refight Plassey as a role-playing campaign, with players representing Siraj himself, his son and son-in-law, the treacherous Mir Jafar, and a few minor princes besides Clive and the British could be represented by a player or controlled by the umpire. If enough players were available, the game could be expanded to cover a larger period of the eighteenth century, with most players taking the roles of Indian leaders and the British, French and possibly Dutch or even Portuguese involved too.

For most of the players, the object of the game is to become Nawab. It is an uphill struggle in a court full of scheming princes and their spies. Your soldiers are loyal to the last person to pay them – and it may not have been you. If fortune smiles on your plots, the throne will be yours, but you will have to reward your followers, players that helped you, and possibly one of the European powers. The Europeans can be useful allies. They have exceptionally loyal soldiers, mighty warships and ready cash. Yet their assistance always seems to come at a price. The exact amount of money in each player's pocket should remain secret, with some suggestion that the Europeans have more money in their warehouses than is really the case. Then Indian rulers short of gold might well be tempted to renege on their agreements and attack the Europeans' factories. Few Indian princes died in their beds; and if they did, it was usually because one of the other occupants had a knife under the pillow. When the time comes, the shrewd player will slip out of the palace one step ahead of the assassins. With your favourite concubine, a few steadfast eunuchs and as many jewels as you can get into a saddle-bag, it's time to head for the hills – literally, only a dash to northern India will take you beyond reach of your enemies. Of course, most escaping Nawabs, like the ill-fated Siraj are betrayed by lowly peasants they have abused in happier times. The only consolation is that your successor, having murdered his way to your throne, is unlikely to live long to profit by it. Mir Jafar's treachery at Plassey availed him nothing in the long run: the British toppled him, only to fall out with his successor, Mir Cossim, an equally rapacious prince with an army of bandits behind him. Yet another war followed...

Designing a Boardgame

Such a role-play game could be administered without too many formal rules by an accomplished umpire, with reasonable knowledge of the period. It has all the makings of a good matrix game, a format explained in several other titles in the Campaign Series. This system, pioneered by Chris Engle in the USA, and by Bob Cordery and others in Britain, has been widely covered in the wargame press. See *The Nugget*, the journal of Wargames Developments, for recent developments.

Alternatively, you could design a far more structured game if you wanted something a little more formal. What I have described here may sound familiar territory to fans of the notorious *Junta*, the best boardgame simulation of current 'banana republic' politics. For a more structured approach, the famous boardgame *Machiavelli* might be a good starting point. Many features of the Italian city state wars are equally applicable to eighteenth century India: plagues, revolts, treachery and bribery. If you employed the same combat system, derived from the classic *Diplomacy*, the European armies should be treated as the double-strength, unbribable Spanish regulars in *Machiavelli*. Otherwise, the basic area movement system, with simultaneous written instructions, should work quite well. Battles will hinge on secret deals struck in smoke-filled tents the night before: but no one will be certain who is on whose side until the battle is well under way.

Another boardgame system that could be applied to the Plassey era is *Kingmaker*, the veteran Wars of the Roses game. Here, the rival royal families are the pawns in a struggle between groups of nobles; the winner is the player who controls the last surviving claimant to the throne and crowns him. The same principle could be applied to the imperial throne in Delhi, with players representing the leading Indian princes.